THE
HOME
STRETCH

GEORGE K.
ILSLEY

THE
HOME
STRETCH

A FATHER,
A SON,
AND
ALL THE THINGS
THEY NEVER TALK ABOUT

ARSENAL PULP PRESS
VANCOUVER

THE HOME STRETCH
Copyright © 2020 by George K. Ilsley

ARSENAL PULP PRESS
Suite 202 – 211 East Georgia St.
Vancouver, BC V6A 1Z6
Canada
arsenalpulp.com

The publisher gratefully acknowledges the support of the Canada Council for the Arts
and the British Columbia Arts Council for its publishing program, and the Government
of Canada, and the Government of British Columbia (through the Book Publishing Tax
Credit Program), for its publishing activities.

Arsenal Pulp Press acknowledges the xʷməθkʷəy̓əm (Musqueam), Sḵwx̱wú7mesh
(Squamish), and səl̓ilwətaʔɬ (Tsleil-Waututh) Nations, custodians of the traditional, ancestral,
and unceded territories where our office is located. We pay respect to their histories,
traditions, and continuous living cultures and commit to accountability, respectful relations,
and friendship.

"Bingo and Black Ice" was published in *subTerrain* #69 as the winner of the 2014 Lush
Triumphant Literary Award for creative non-fiction.

Front cover design by Oliver McPartlin
Cover photograph by Felipe Cardoso, courtesy of Pexels
Full cover and text design by Jazmin Welch
Edited by Shirarose Wilensky
Proofread by Alison Strobel

Printed and bound in Canada

Library and Archives Canada Cataloguing in Publication:
Title: The home stretch : a father, a son, and all the things they never talk about /
George K. Ilsley.
Names: Ilsley, George K., 1958– author.
Identifiers: Canadiana (print) 20190232706 | Canadiana (ebook) 20190232765 |
ISBN 9781551527956 (softcover) | ISBN 9781551527963 (HTML)
Subjects: LCSH: Ilsley, George K., 1958– | LCSH: Ilsley, George K., 1958-—Family. |
LCSH: Fathers and sons—Canada—Biography. | LCSH: Aging parents—Canada—
Biography. | CSH: Authors, Canadian (English)—Biography. | LCGFT: Autobiographies.
Classification: LCC PS8567.L74 Z46 2020 | DDC C818/.603—dc23

Dedicated to my parents,
Christina and Stephen

CONTENTS

When you don't have obsession, when you don't have hang-up, when you don't have inhibition, when you are not afraid that you will be breaking certain rules, when you are not afraid that you will not fulfill somebody's expectations—what more enlightenment do you want? That's it.

—Dzongsar Khyentse Rinpoche,
Words of My Perfect Teacher

1

THE OUTSIDE
WORLD

MY FATHER CLIMBS THE STAIRS FROM THE GARAGE, one step at time. He clomps into the kitchen, where I am putting away the groceries, and braces himself up on the dishwasher.

He is sputtering mad.

"If you're going to be like that," he says, "I'm never going shopping with you again!"

In the fall of 2010, my father is ninety-one years old.

On the first day of my visit, after cleaning the kitchen in the morning, I take my father in the van to go up town. His fridge is almost empty, and I want to stock up on essentials, like extra-virgin olive oil and fresh ginger.

My father uses cloth bags for shopping. The bags used to be a novelty, and originally were plain white cotton, with the name of the grocery store in big blue letters. The store was sold, yet Dad is careful not to use the Moody's bag at the other store: the one that was the competition to the old Moody's. He pays attention to which bag to use at which store, even though no one would care, but does not notice his reusable cloth bags are disgusting. He never thinks to wash them. Grocery clerks recoil at the sight of the dark-stained relics Dad brings out to use. When I see the state of the rank old bags Dad slips off the door handle for our grocery trip, I flat-out refuse to touch them.

"Those need to be washed, Dad. We'll have to use plastic today."

"What's wrong with them?" He genuinely does not seem to know.

"Well, for one thing, they smell really bad. We can't use these for food. When was the last time you washed them?"

"Oh," he says. "Last week."

Last week is Dad's answer for everything. I don't know if he really believes "last week" or if it is just an answer he has come up with to put people off. It sure sounds more reassuring than "I don't know." Most people would be satisfied with his response.

Most annoying people, with questions.

Like me.

And yes, it's true. We used to buy our groceries at a store called Moody's.

Moody Brothers, it was. And then just Moody's.

In my own life I'm in the habit of shopping for food all the time, so we don't buy all that much on this first trip. Just enough to get started.

When we get back to the house, I slide open the side door of the van and gather up the groceries.

Dad says, "Give me some of those."

I grab all the bags. "It's okay, Dad. I got them."

The load is not that heavy, considering I am only going from the van to the house. I'm used to walking a couple of blocks or more and lugging everything.

So I huff all the groceries up the stairs from the garage.

I set the bags down in the kitchen. Carrots and celery make their home in the crisper of the freshly cleaned fridge. Cans of organic BPA-free beans go into the "current corner" of the pantry. Much shelf space in the pantry is cluttered with convenience foods and baking supplies—Shake 'n Bake, cake mixes, rock-hard bags of brown sugar. The pantry is still very much the domain of my mother, an enthusiastic baker, who died more than twenty years ago.

This really needs to be cleaned out. But can't do everything the first day.

And here is when Dad catches up with me in the kitchen, sputtering mad. He leans against the dishwasher, catching his breath, his eyes sparking. "If you're going to be like that," he declares, "I'm never going shopping with you again!"

What? What did I do?

I know I'm fussy with groceries; I've always been very particular about what I will eat and what I won't. I'll be doing the cooking while I'm here, so I feel empowered to do things my way. I know what I'm like, how impossible, so when we go shopping I buy the groceries. Paying gives me the freedom to get what I want, and my penny-pinching father has no reason to get upset.

We no longer fight at the grocery store. We don't end up arguing over crackers. I just directly and simply express myself: "I want it, I'm going to buy it." And so I buy two kinds—the old-school sal-tines Dad considers synonymous with "crackers" and the Triscuits

I prefer. Dad likes Triscuits, too, but the price on them is terrible. They're not even on sale.

"We'll just get both," I said, "and then we can stop talking about crackers."

But that is not what got Dad going. That is not why he is breathless and angry. Finally he is able to tell me.

"You didn't let me help with the bags," he says. "I have to do things like that to stay strong."

I am going to have to learn to be more diplomatic. I thought I was helping, just grabbing all the bags myself. But perhaps I made it look too easy, made it too obvious I didn't need Dad's help. I made the decisions, paid for everything, and carried all the bags—what was he there for?

He too is used to doing things himself, and cannot bear to be sidelined.

I'll have to be more careful not to offend his new-found vanity. Be more aware of my father's special needs. A couple of decades ago, if I grabbed all the groceries and hustled into the house, he would not have batted an eye. He would have just hurried ahead to unlock the door for me.

Of course, he also would have been driving.

Today, I was driving, I carried all the groceries, and I hurried ahead to unlock the door for him.

Who knew it was so easy to offend just by being helpful?

———

I CAN SEE HOW AGING might make my father feel more sensitive. I can see how age makes my father disappear, and become something no longer quite as real. He is no longer just a man—he is an old man, either patronized or ignored. I watch what happens during encounters with strangers. He has become insignificant in their eyes—if he is even noticed at all.

Already I can feel the cloak of invisibility growing strong around me, in my own life, such as when I find myself on public transit with a group of young people. Even if one of them happens to glance at me, I do not register. The cloak of invisibility is a superpower my ego struggles to appreciate. The writer/eavesdropper in me loves it, because I have become a fly on the wall. But my resilient-yet-fragile ego bristles at being so frankly, so obviously, so automatically judged as irrelevant.

A fly on the wall has a vantage point, yes, but is excluded from the group.

My father and my brother live together. My brother has been renovating the house, and the disruption has Dad feeling unsettled. He expects everything to get back to normal soon.

What does my ninety-one-year-old father expect normal to be?

In the meantime, Dad's ego has decided to fight back. There is no going gently into that good night for him. He may be depressed, and lonely, but he has not given up. He remains a staunch contrarian. He is still stubborn and feisty.

If anything, his wounded pride has provoked him into being even more domineering. Like a cornered, desperate animal, he is prone to lash out with whatever annoying weapons he has left.

———

MY FATHER'S HOUSE IS A FIVE-LEVEL SPLIT-LEVEL that he had built. Only the shell was done when we moved in. Dad did the rest himself, mostly, as I recall. Mom did the nagging, so she did her part—or else things would never have been finished. She did a lot of work, too, painting and cleaning, and when my mother did something she told you all about it.

I helped shingle the roof. Can that really be true?

My father tells this story. It is the only compliment he has for me in his quiver. He likes to tell people how impressed the contractors were the summer we built the house.

One of the contractors told my father he never saw kids work so hard.

My brother was twelve. I was ten. Like monkeys we were, scrambling up and down ladders, fetching things, hammering on the roof.

A five-level split-level sounds massive but the house never felt that big, not even when I was little. But five levels does mean stairs everywhere you go. From the garage, there are stairs down to the basement and up to the main floor. From the main floor, up to the bathroom and bedrooms, and then more stairs up to the top floor, where the kids slept.

Four flights of stairs connect the five levels.

It wasn't just the house that struggled to get built. My father's projects often remained unfinished. The shell of a plywood catamaran sprawled in the garage for years, always in the way. Long slender bamboo poles intended to be converted into fishing rods cluttered the basement in our first house, then followed us when we moved and spent the last forty years taking up space in a garden shed, where they must be pushed aside in every search for something actually useful.

Most of my projects are less cumbersome but no less unfinished.

———

IF I USE THE WORD "HOME" I almost always mean Nova Scotia.

Home is my parents' home. Which is ironic, since growing up there all I wanted to do was leave. Get out of there and start a real life somewhere better.

On the outside.

It feels like a prison, in a way, the family home. It is my father's home now, where he lives with my brother. The current inmates of the family home are not speaking to each other.

A visit to my father's house feels like an imprisonment suspended in time and space—some things change but the craving for something else never disappears. This is a place I couldn't wait to leave. Of course, I was young then. So very young that I still believed in a geographic cure.

From Nova Scotia it is only possible to go west, and I went to Toronto, dawdling there for fifteen-odd years. I left Toronto several times. The secret to leaving Toronto is to move away more times than you move back. I moved to Montreal a couple of times, which was great but never really worked out. And then, in 1995, I moved to Vancouver.

Vancouver is as far away from Nova Scotia as you can possibly get, almost, and this is where I live. Having hit the ocean, I can go no farther. Vancouver is a place of permanent spring and then permanent fall; the two major seasons briefly interrupted, perhaps, by whimsical suggestions of something very much like summer or winter. Most Canadians who visit Vancouver are unable to locate any weather resembling winter—not without driving to a nearby mountain. That is the most miraculous thing about life in Vancouver as a Canadian—one can look up and see winter whenever you like. Winter is something you drive to if you want, instead of being a nuisance all around you, becoming tiresome, and dominating an entire season. Winter is visited, rather than lived in.

It is not so terrible visiting the birthplace—it is just that I feel so displaced, and unseen. All the overwhelming muck from my youth surges up so eagerly, threatening to engulf me, to drag me under and bury me alive.

It is not so terrible, not such an ordeal—and yet somehow it is.

I end up watching loads of television.

I don't live with a television because I fear it is a big time-wasting distraction. I am old enough to remember when television was talked about as a form of brainwashing and social conditioning using subliminal messaging—but that is rarely mentioned any-more. Did the brainwashing potential just disappear? Perhaps the programming has been thoughtful enough to reassure viewers, help them forget all that nonsense about brainwashing and subliminal messages.

When I visit my father I fall into the abyss. My entire world disappears into this abyss. My life instantly becomes unreal and I watch endless TV in an attempt to fill the void. Even though I vow to turn it off at midnight, I stay up half the night, my schedule thrown out of whack by the four-hour time difference. Going to bed at midnight in Nova Scotia is pointless when my body thinks it's only eight o'clock.

Despite the sheer number of channels from Dad's satellite dish, there is not much variety. Most shows feels like an imitation of another program.

There is such a thing as a tennis channel, and this is a gift from the obsession deities. How did they know? I've been playing tennis in Vancouver, mostly doubles in a social league, and it's impossible to find doubles tennis on television—except on Tennis Channel.

Dad starts to watch tennis too, especially after I outline the rules. He has trouble seeing the ball, though, with his cataracts, so I have to explain a lot. I'm happy to answer tennis questions. I never realized how subtly complicated the game of tennis was until I tried to explain it to my father. At least he asks questions about tennis.

I often think of my father when I survey the mess of unfinished projects strewn around my desk, arrayed in layers like an archeological site. My father's unfinished projects are something you trip over; mine collect just as much dust but are easier to push aside into their own special file folder and never look at again.

When I visit my father in Nova Scotia, I do not mention my unfinished projects.

My father shows no interest in my life, so I do not say very much about Vancouver, my job, or my friends.

Every time I visit my father (and before that, my parents) I remember, *Oh yeah, this is what it is like*. It's like *The Simpsons*. Homer's father, Abraham Simpson, lives in a seniors' home. At the entrance to the home is a sign:

THANK YOU
FOR NOT
DISCUSSNG
THE
OUTSIDE
WORLD

The inverse of the outside world is the inside world—the world of feelings and intuition, of memory and childhood. Visiting my father is always a trip to my inside world, a trip to the past, a trip to my childhood, a trip to my mother who died in 1987, a trip to a place where my own paper-thin life in Vancouver is out of reach and never mentioned.

And so, in these pages, I will not be discussing the outside world.

————

MY FATHER HAS LIVED IN THE SMALL TOWN OF BERWICK, Nova Scotia, for almost his entire life. He was born on one corner of Main and Commercial (in the place known as the Early house after the family who lived there for generations) and then grew up across the street in a sprawling Victorian home with bay windows, a parlour used for storage, and a second staircase, steep and narrow, that led up to little rooms above the kitchen. One of these little rooms was my father's old bedroom, still littered during my childhood with the debris of his ham radio hobby. Pinned to the rough walls, QSL cards confirmed contact with other radio operators around the world.

I loved my grandparents' house, which no longer exists. It is still a place I visit in my dreams. It is the only home of my childhood I miss: the one that is no longer there.

My father's early fascination with radios led to his career. During the Second World War he trained as an electrician and installed electrical systems in airplanes. After the war, he continued as an electrician, wiring houses as power lines extended throughout the countryside. For good measure, Dad was also a plumber. My father never lacked for work because he was not the sort of person who could bring himself to ask for payment. He would install an electrical entrance, buying the materials himself, and come home with a box of apples. Berwick calls itself the Apple Capital of Nova Scotia, and there were always wooden crates of apples in our basement cold room. Red Delicious in those days were perfectly named (but a bugger to pick, because the stem had to be left in), and I loved

Golden Russets, a small golden amber apple with skin rough to the touch like a potato and flesh sweet to the taste like a crunchy pear. I often ate two or three of these rough little sweet Russets at a time. Whatever I could grab with my small, greedy hands.

My mother was the social organizer in the family. After I left home, she telephoned at least once a week, usually waking me up, and talked about their garden, their greenhouse, their weather, and their teenage Siamese cat. The possibility of dramatic events reverberating through my own young life was barely hinted at and certainly never discussed. It was best just to avoid uncomfortable topics.

Now the silence is absolute. My father asks no questions. I've had the same job in Vancouver for fifteen years—my father has no idea what I do. I've had two books of fiction published—my father has never mentioned them or indicated he is aware that I write, even though I might be seen in the evening at the dining room table doing that very thing.

Several years ago I showed Dad an anthology edited by Susan Musgrave, with two old manual typewriters on the cover.

He held it cautiously. "Are you in here?" he asked.

My short story "When Parrots Bark" was written in the first person and opened with this sentence: *"What good's a parrot who can't even talk?" my father asks again, just to bug me.*

My father managed to read only the one line before he stopped. "I never said that," he declared.

"It's fiction, Dad," I protested.

My father did not dare read any further.

If I brandish a book that includes a piece of my writing, virtually everyone can manage a few enthusiastic noises. My father merely grunted at the sight of this anthology, grunted like he did when I was trying to get him to do me a favour that he already knew was going to be too much work. He grunted, read one sentence, declared it false, and set the book down next to his chair—where it would still languish to this day if I had not retrieved it to deploy as a "praise me" prop in more fertile fields.

Where, I have to say, it worked like a charm.

———

IT'S LIBERATING HAVING A MOTHER WHO DIED. It's much easier to write about people who are not alive and can never be offended.

I can write about Mom and not worry about pissing her off—or how I was going to manage to be able to deal with her.

There's a lot of my mother in my early short fiction. When I read that collection now I'm surprised how much is flat-out memoir—but then just veers off into the safety and convenience of clear fiction. Writing about my mother felt urgent—I needed to get some sort of handle on her, and her overwhelming influence, and write her out of my system.

I wrote about my mother in fiction, but I'd invent the father figure, make him the cruel drinker. If I wrote about a domineering mother and a drunk father—that was all Mom. She was big enough, and complex enough, to split her in two, in fiction, and make her both mother and father. The bullying, the bossiness, all that love, all that drinking—Mom did it all, and gave me so much to write about. And then when she died so suddenly, she freed up all that material.

My parents also gave me the gift of shame, so it took a long time to appreciate all I had been given. Only after I grew older did I begin to realize that my family of origin may not have had a lot of material wealth, but my parents did give me a wealth of material.

It also took me ages to figure out I had abandonment issues because when I was growing up my parents were always there. How could I have been abandoned? Dad was never absent, but he lived in his own world. He was controlling, too, if you let him. I avoided most of that by moving away. I moved out of his control.

But now I am back. Back in his house and in his world and banging up against his walls. All the old walls I remember and new walls I'm only just discovering by running into them face first.

I never wrote about my father in fiction. Partly because he's still alive and partly because he just never really got under my skin like my mother did. When my mother was alive, my father's ability to be truly annoying was overshadowed.

My father and I never overlapped in quite the same way Mom and I did—at least not as adults. After I left the house, our relations were friendly, but distant. He doesn't want to know anything about my life, and that is naturally distancing.

As long as we were distant and I left him alone, we got along just fine.

Only now, as my father enters his nineties, having outlived my mother by more than twenty years, and my aspirations of eldercare become more interventionist, has our relationship had a chance to deepen.

And by deepen, I mean really begin to annoy each other.

That's what families do.

———

DAD DID SHOW SOME INTEREST IN MY LIFE after I went to Dawson City. I was in the Yukon for three and a half months starting in October 2007 as the writer-in-residence at Berton House Writers'

Retreat. For the life of me I do not know why more Canadians don't look north when making travel plans.

My father never said anything when I told him I was going to Berton House. Only after I came back, if I mentioned having been up north, did he say, "I wish I had known you were going—I would have visited you."

He has said this many times—*I wish I had known*—without ever once acknowledging why I went to Dawson City, or that I might have been busy. It was, after all, a working trip. But then—my work in the outside world is invisible to him. And maybe his entire retroactive plan was so hypothetical that logistics did not matter. My father was eighty-eight when I went north, and getting there from Nova Scotia would have been expensive, and not quick. It's hard to imagine Dad being willing to spend thousands of dollars and two days of travel each way to go anywhere.

The other thing is, I've lived in Vancouver for many years. People come from all over to see this city, considered one of the world's most beautiful, and to enjoy the spectacular natural grandeur of its surroundings. Vancouver is a city now more likely to delight tourists than comfort its residents, so it can be, weather permitting, the perfect place to visit. Dad has never suggested visiting Vancouver, which is just as exotic as the Yukon if you've never been. Southern British Columbia is basically Canada's Mediterranean coast, with palm trees and a notable lack of winter—a balmy setting surrounded by a vigil of snow-capped peaks.

But he was not visiting me, in his imaginary trip to Dawson City—it was the Yukon that seized him. And gosh, he could have gone at any time in his life if he was that keen.

But now, you see, the way Dad tells the story it's my fault he never went. Because I didn't tell him I was going.

Dawson City used to be almost completely isolated by winter. Most warm-season travel was by riverboat, and the trip out of Dawson was called "going outside." The fall, just before freeze-up, was the last chance to "go outside" before spring breakup six months later.

Dawson was "here" and everywhere else in the world was "outside."

In these pages, the outside trip in the spring and in the fall is going home to small-town Nova Scotia to visit my father. On the flight east, somewhere in what might be, at that altitude, remnants of Upper Canada, my outside world drops away, is of no more relevance to this story, and will barely be mentioned.

My inside world, on the other hand, is something I cannot stop talking about.

I always call it "going home." Even though I have not lived in Nova Scotia since 1979, it is "home."

It used to be that visiting Dad meant going home for a week, which was as short a time as I dared.

Each stretch of time at home feels like a prison sentence— locked up with my father and sequestered from my outside world. Counting the days until I am to be released, set free—free to do all the things I feel to be impossible while confined within my father's dusty, cluttered house.

So, it is 2010. My father is ninety-one years old. My life sentence goes something like this: me, my father, and the blurry line that divides us, or defines us, or maybe doesn't even exist.

At the beginning of each trip home, the time stretches long, so long. And then at the end I can't believe there is only one more night. One last night to feel and try to hang on to. My emotions betray any adherence to logic—I am sad to arrive and sad to leave. Usually, though, once I am back in the air —(soaring)— I feel a sense of possibility. I taste the rush of the jet stream. I feel the power of escaping gaining strength, like a vampire feeding on the imagined glories of the outside world.

This is something I know very well. Escape is an old friend.

2

WEDNESDAY NIGHT
POLKA PARTY

*Furniture Surfing: Navigating through the home
holding on to whatever is available to provide support—
from the table to the back of a chair to the counter,
from the buffet to the door frame, and so on.*

"WHY DIDN'T YOU EVER DANCE WITH MOM?"

I surprise myself by voicing this question, but I've been wondering. My father, in his nineties, has become obsessed with dancing. His mobility is not great (it's not even good), but he refuses to use a cane because "it makes me look old." In the house he furniture surfs, but outside crossing the yard on his way to my brother's store to pick up the newspaper, he leans forward and to the right so badly that if he stopped tootling along he would fall right over. Bent sharply towards his destination, he shuffles crisp little baby steps in his enormous old heavy workboots, laces undone. Passersby pause to watch, questioning whether to intervene, until he arrives at something solid to hold on to, and everyone relaxes.

This is the man who has discovered dancing.

Dad's favourite television station, scooped up by satellite dish, is from the American heartland. He enjoys programs about vintage tractors, cowboy gospel music, horse-drawn plow competitions, and steam locomotives on narrow-gauge railways. He plans his week around what he calls "my show"—a dance party with polka bands on the stage and geriatric white couples circling the room. His show only has a couple of cameras and very little jumping between them. The music is upbeat and the presentation so slow and simple Dad can follow it. Relaxing in his recliner chair, he bobs his feet to the oompah tempo.

"Now that's dancing," my father says. "Those are some good dancers, aren't they?"

He waits for my response.

"Huh, George? Aren't they?" he asks again, and seems satisfied with my half-hearted grunt.

Later we watch my choice of program—*So You Think You Can Dance*. These dancers are young, scantily clad, racially diverse, and almost supernaturally athletic. They must avoid being eliminated by dancing their hearts out—hip hop, ballroom, cha-cha, contemporary. My father seems offended by the acrobatic performances.

"That's not dancing," he scoffs.

I suspect he simply can't follow the program because there are endless camera angles and fast-paced jumps. The editing is frenetic and the show scrambles in his brain. It's also past his bedtime and he's mostly asleep in his chair. Before long, he wakes up and scuffs into the kitchen for his pills and then off to bed. I hold my breath every time he crosses the middle of a room, where there is no counter or furniture to steady him. He wears a sweater in the house, and at nighttime, before going upstairs, he leaves it in the living room on the chesterfield. On his way to bed, he waves good night to me by opening and closing one hand, a child's wave, and then staggers across the living room, wrestling with his ratty old sweater, losing his balance. I lean forward, my heart gulping in my ears as he stumbles past the coffee table towards the brick fireplace.

Every night it's the same thing. He almost falls, but does no more than alarm me. I do the same thing, too, every time. I have a fresh new panic attack as he lurches closer to the unforgiving red-brick fireplace, his arms snared behind him.

But let's get back to my question. "Why didn't you ever dance with Mom?"

My father requires no time to reflect before he answers.

"She wouldn't dance with me," he explains.

He says this casually, confidently, without hesitation. Perhaps he has forgotten who he is talking to: not a store clerk, or bank teller or another near-stranger who agrees with everything my father says but knows precious little about his life except the stories he tells. Perhaps he has forgotten that I actually grew up with him and my mother, and have my own memories. I have my own axe to grind.

She wouldn't dance with him! I flash back to a series of scenes, lots of sad little parties, my mother embarrassingly lively, my father a stick-in-the-mud. Of course, Mom was usually half-cut, and Dad never drank.

My poor dear mother, bless her soul, was naturally fun loving, but if she was drinking her mood was amiable only while on its way up. It was no small chore dealing with the cruel, sullen, crying mess when she crashed back down.

When feeling especially frantic and jolly, she'd get all dolled up in a long dress and long earrings, pull out a pair of cheap plastic strappy dancing shoes, and drench herself in harsh cologne—trying to make an occasion out of next to nothing.

Trying to make her life bearable.

Crank up the Charley Pride ("Kiss an Angel Good Mornin' ..."), stomp her hard little heels around the living room, reeking of a bitter chemical blossom.

("... And love her like the devil when you get back home.")

Tug at my father's arm, begging him to dance with her.

He'd most likely say, "Not right now."

Not now, in Dad-ese, meant no. If he came right out and said no, we would say, "Why not?" and pester the hell out of him. So he said, "Not now" instead, but we all knew what it really meant.

Mom turned her fevered gaze to me, her fists and elbows dancing in front of her face. I was the surrogate spouse, as I have learned to describe it. There was unboundaried bonding between Mom and me. There was emotional incest, a term I've only just recently heard. When one parent (my father) is emotionally unavailable, the other parent (my mother) turns to a child with a torrent of unmet emotional needs. I became my mother's best friend. I listened to her complaints and her problems. I was her youngest child and her therapist. I lived right inside the very heart of their dysfunctional marriage—which, for a child, is like living inside a volcano. The exposure to so much heat and pressure is too much for an ordinary young mortal, and this is how a "hero child" is forged. Well I rose to the challenge. I danced with my mother. I danced with her when she was sober and alone, and I danced with her when she was drunk and no one else would.

This is what I remember—"Heartaches by the Number"—and being cajoled into dancing with my mother, because Dad was never willing.

"But Dad," I say, "what about all those parties? Mom always wanted to dance, and ended up dancing with me, lots of times, while you just sat in the chair."

He looks at me, bewildered, as if he honestly doesn't have a clue what I am going on about. He believes his own memories and everyone else is "full of baloney."

I guess we have that in common.

Except I don't say "baloney."

No one ever called my mother an alcoholic—that is, no one but me. I like to think my view of her, even though she's been dead for many years, is nuanced and accurate. I display no bias when I suggest Mom has not become a saint just by managing to stay dead for a couple of decades. I'll be the first to describe her as a nag or a control freak, if the topic comes up.

My father, though, only remembers the good things.

Unless it is convenient to find someone to blame for his own actions.

"She wouldn't dance with me."

When Dad gives me this simple answer, I feel a familiar sensation: a wall closing off my chest, moving up, and blocking my throat. I recognize this wall—all the unfelt emotions are on the other side of it. It is like a dam, and when it breaks, there is an ugly torrent. It is also like a firewall, designed for safety, and if it fails all hell breaks loose.

I grew up with this sensation in my body, and it resurrects in a flash with my father's simple crazy-wrong answer to my question. The flash is anger and the fuel is frustration. The power of this surge speaks to the depths of frustration still lingering under my skin. Still living in my flesh after all these years.

When feelings can't be expressed they bury themselves. I shouldn't be surprised at what hardness keeps surfacing, like rocks every spring when you till the field.

My wall grew in response to another wall: my father's. My father's wall said things like "Because I said so" and expected that to end all discussion. My wall grew because my feelings did not have a voice and instead found their nourishment within my own body, like sulky little parasites, subsisting on petty resentments and festering slights.

I am angry and I know I am angry and that is why I push it. "But Dad, what about all those parties?"

He just looks at me like I am an idiot.

This, too, is familiar.

My father and I have lots of little tiffs and arguments now. I'm quite blunt about things I never before had a chance to say.

"Remember that time you beat me with the rake handle when I was finishing up the lawn and you wanted me to stop what I was doing and go work in the garden? You treated us kids like mindless slaves."

No, of course he does not remember beating me with the rake. He dismisses my story with a blanket denial. "We never raked the lawn."

"*You* didn't!" Oh how indignant I am! "I certainly raked. I mowed and raked. All fucking summer."

It's quite sporting, I find, almost recreational, arguing with a ninety-one-year-old. We butt heads, I get stuff off my chest, he huffs and puffs and then dozes off.

He takes a nap, reboots, and that's that. When he wakes up, he has no memory we just quarrelled.

For much of my life, I resented that my father was largely oblivious to my vast and turbulent emotional landscape. Now I am relieved at his lack of interest and, frankly, enjoying the liberty to express myself without worrying he is going to hit the roof, stop talking to me, or kick me out of his house.

There is a series of public service announcements on television about elder abuse. Every time one appears I feel guilty. We watch these elder abuse PSAs and I wonder what on earth Dad could be thinking. Adult children are depicted saying horrible things to elderly parents and the stern message from the Canadian government is that this is unacceptable. There is a number to call. Dad never reaches for the phone, so maybe I can share my hurt feelings and bitter judgments even more freely. At this rate, I'll soon be rid of all my lingering resentments—as long as I don't cross the line as far as the 1-800 number.

Our little quarrels release some of the bottled-up pressure, even if nothing is resolved. Dad is ninety-one, almost ninety-two—my constant companion is the thought: *It's now or never.*

In a way, I don't care that he doesn't recall beating me with the rake. My achievement is to open my mouth and speak up—speaking my truth about experiences that have left me scarred.

This radical act (sharing, as some call it) is a departure from what I was able to do as a child, and represents a step towards the possibility of having a real relationship with my father. This possibility is what I hope to live with after he is gone. I want to have at least done my part in our awkward dance down memory lane.

There are all kinds of loose ends and dangling frayed bits. I seize a quiet moment one afternoon to initiate the following exchange:

"You know, Dad," I say, "I can't remember you ever saying that you loved me."

He looks at me, his hooded eyes slowly blinking. His lower lids droop, sagging away from his cloudy eyes. Gravity is winning its long relentless battle.

"I was just thinking, you know—I've never heard you say, 'I love you.' To this day, I don't even know if you do or not."

The silence in the room roars.

"Of course," I say, "I'm fifty years old. I don't need to be told."

He clears his throat.

"I would say that I do," he declares, somewhat formally.

Sometimes my father's reserve is insufferable, his emotions so diffuse, so distant, that our small moments produce an equally small measure of satisfaction. To squeeze meaning from his words, one might extract something like: *If I was forced to think about whether I loved my youngest child and had to say something on this uncomfortable topic, I suppose that* I would say that I do *love you, George.*

He did not say all that, of course, but a generous-minded listener might wring such great splashy gobs of meaning from his spongy little sentence.

However, given my literal nature, I cannot help but note that Dad has still never said to me those three simple words: *I love you.*

He said six words. He managed to say "I" twice.

But not "love."

And not "you."

———

MY FATHER WAS BORN IN THIS SMALL TOWN in the Annapolis Valley and, except for during the war (which to his generation means the Second World War), has lived here his entire life.

Everyone in town knows my father by name.

"How are you, Stephen?"

"Fair to worse," he used to say. Now he says, "I'm still here."

"That's good, Stephen."

Here's the thing my ninety-odd-year-old father does not seem to grasp. When people talk to him, they pretend to be more interested than they really are. They are being polite, and he thinks their interest is genuine.

Or perhaps I am the one who is confused. Perhaps all these down-home types are both polite and genuine.

Their politeness, however, presents an opportunity and cracks open the door just far enough for Dad to make the first step towards one of his current obsessions. His mission is to find a woman to come over on Wednesday night to enjoy his polka program with him.

My father is on a quest. He needs a dance partner so his recent obsession with dancing can take a huge leap forward into a whole new dimension—and magically blossom into actually dancing.

At the drugstore he tells the cashier about his show—the polka party with the lively music.

"I never used to have the music in me," Dad says, "but this program is terrific."

He repeats the word "terrific" for emphasis. "Terrific" is his go-to word to confer the highest praise, and the hard syllables fetch up in his dentures and lend a faint wet rattle to his loose upper plate.

"Sounds like quite the show, Stephen," the cashier says.

She smiles at both my father and me, her eyes glowing behind her large glasses. I forget her name. She's friendly with me, too, when I pop into the drugstore on one of the endless eldercare errands. The feeling sometimes in a small town is that everyone is a freelance social worker. When I was growing up here and overwhelmed with all my own crap (then a mysterious hydra-headed monster but, as it turns out, mostly internalized homophobia), I feared everyone was nosy and judgmental. Now while visiting my father, whose own father was born in the 1880s (the nineteenth century!) in this same small town, everyone feels *connected*.

Everyone knows who I am ("the other son, who lives in Vancouver"), and no one says boo to me, except "How's your father doing?" and "How are you doing?" and "How long you home for?"

Times have changed, but I am also a different person.

With both hands pressed flat on the drugstore counter, Dad pushes himself a little more upright and leans towards the cashier to ask his important question. "Do you want to come over on Wednesday and we can dance?"

"That sounds like fun, Stephen." The cashier appears enthusiastic, but her tone signals there's absolutely no way this is ever going to happen. She giggles at the thought. "Can I bring my husband?"

"Okay, yes," Dad says. "But he will have to bring another woman—if he wants someone to dance with."

The cashier and I both burst out laughing.

"Well now," she says. "It's a date."

She is humouring him, and this makes me uncomfortable. I'm not sure how sophisticated my father's social skills used to be, when he was in his prime and I was an oblivious child, but now he is unable to see when people are joking. Dad really will expect her to show up on Wednesday.

That is, if he remembers.

Dad has more or less the same conversation with a lot of women. He casts his net widely in his quest for a dance partner. His type is no more discernible than this—any woman he is able to detain long enough to ask. These women are invariably polite, if lying to an old man is considered polite.

Some find a way to say no: "Thanks, Stephen, but my grandchildren are visiting and I have to bake cookies!" or, "Sorry, did you say Wednesday? Oh, I have a class that night."

Many, however, laughingly agree to come over on Wednesday night to enjoy the polka party with him.

None ever do.

————

WHEN DAD IS OUT HE IS LOOKING FOR A DANCE PARTNER, but in his own home he is distracted by the renovations.

My brother is attempting some upgrades and this is causing tension. The windows have mostly been replaced. The top floor, where my old bedroom used to be, has been gutted and re-insulated, and now has drywall instead of the wood panelling still throughout the rest of the house. That wood panelling everywhere made my mother say she felt like she was living in prison.

The top floor still needs plaster and paint, but the new insulation means cold drafts from above are a thing of the past. My father, however, is still convinced there is a problem. He's very attached to the curtains installed across the stairs on the same floor as his bedroom.

These curtains, originally goldenesque, have faded to a calf-shit yellow and the cracked rubber backing is flaking. My mother whipped up these pleated curtains on her Singer sewing machine. Now about forty years old, they have not been washed for the last twenty-five. When installed, they didn't quite reach the floor, so Dad rigged up a wire extender for each curtain hook. Improvised wire extensions for these sad old curtains really complete the look of ruin and dilapidation.

The golden curtains used to sweep the length of the landing, extending across the top of one flight and the bottom of the other. The curtains across the stairs going up to the top floor were taken down at some point. My brother got tired of batting them aside. Or did I remove them, as a preliminary skirmish in a larger battle? I have a vague memory of declaring they needed to be washed, and then not putting them back up. Dad never made as much fuss about that set of curtains. But the other set, across the top of the stairs down to the main floor, remains a battlefront where my father has drawn the line.

Every time you pass through you are supposed to adjust the curtains behind you. They must be closed at all times to prevent cold air from coming down the stairs, whipping through the kitchen, and pooling around Dad's feet in the living room. He is fanatical about this, and will get upset if they are left open even an inch. Straight down the stairs from the curtains is the kitchen door and this too must be "closed"—which in this case means it should be almost but not entirely closed. It must be carefully adjusted to remain open about two inches. Even though it is a door we go through a hundred times a day, it must never be left wide open, lest the draft whip through unchecked. And it must never be closed completely because that sends the icy breeze directly to Dad's feet in the living room, before it even has a chance to mellow a bit in the kitchen.

While ensconced in his living room chair, Dad will ask six times in an evening, "Is the kitchen door closed?"

I'll answer yes whether it is or not, because honestly, I don't think it makes any difference. But I am sly enough to make sure on my next trip to the kitchen that the door is adjusted to official standards before my father catches on that I lied to him.

When we moved into this house in 1968, it was unfinished and the only source of heat was the wood-burning fireplace in the living room. Although the very picture of cozy warmth, a fireplace can suck the heat out of a room and send it up the chimney.

The result, at that time, was cold air pouring down the stairs and hot air rushing out the chimney.

"I'd never build another split level," Dad says. "Too drafty."

The cold bite Dad still feels comes from a lack of insulation in the crawl space directly above his head as he sits in his corner of the living room, but there's nothing to be gained trying to point out the obvious or the logical. He made up his mind years ago and his conclusions are cemented into place. Dad focuses all his diligence on the curtains and the kitchen door. I have seen him many times climb the stairs just to adjust the curtains disturbed less than an inch by someone passing through.

A humble sheet of unadorned cardboard now blocks the fireplace, preventing warm air in the room escaping up the chimney. I can't remember the last time we had a cozy fire. We went from using the fireplace all the time to never being allowed to use it anymore because it was inefficient. But back when the fireplace was in use, the curtains on the stairs not only prevented cold air coming down, but also kept the heat on the main floor. There was no need for warmth to reach the top floor of the house, where only the children slept. Why waste wood trying to heat the top floor just for the kids?

The major conflict between my brother and my father during the renovations is that my brother imagined it might be possible to clean up some of the decades of clutter in the garage. He imagined throwing things into the garbage, or recycling.

What happens with home renovations is something like a domino effect. The current project is turning the laundry room on the main level into a bathroom. The washer and dryer are to move to the garage, where space needed to be freed up. So Dad was asked to consider letting go of some of his stuff.

My father was an electrician and a plumber but has long since retired. However, "retired" is probably too definitive a word for how Dad views his situation. He never really retired—he just took on less work. Although he has not done much work in twenty years (and none in the last how many), he believes he might start working again at any moment and needs to be prepared. Therefore, everything must be left just the way it was.

Let's not even bother trying to point out that a lot of his supplies are no longer suitable for new building codes. Let's not mention that he has been holding on to some of the junk for thirty or forty years for no good reason. Don't you dare mention that Dad is certainly never going to work again.

I hear all about these heated discussions. Not much gets cleaned out of the garage because every single thing requires at least twenty minutes of arguing before it is replaced on the shelf and something even more obviously useless prompts a fresh round of arguing.

Oh believe me, I have heard all about this.

"Your brother threw out all my stuff," Dad says.

"Garage still looks jam-packed to me."

"A lot of valuable things," Dad says. "He threw them all away."

"How valuable?"

Dad thinks, before coming up with a number. "One hundred dollars." He pronounces the amount with some gravity, like he expects me to be impressed.

"Okay," I say, after listening several times to my father's complaint. "How about I give you one hundred dollars? If I gave you a hundred dollars will you get over it and let it go and stop talking about it?"

Dad does not want the hundred dollars. It is not about the money.

Then what is it about?

He wants the past, just like it always was or at least how he prefers to remember it. He wants to hang on to it, and never let it go. That is what he really wants, and nothing else will satisfy.

The garage stored the remnants of my father's work life. Dad half believes, in his hazy way, that he can pick up work again if he chooses. There is no way he can accept that his work life is completely behind him.

My brother is also an electrician, so nothing useful was discarded. Most of Dad's stuff remains in the garage, not worth fighting about. Dad is a hoarder to one degree or another. He was a teenager in the 1930s, a creature of the Great Depression, and does not throw things away.

Lately, on his walks he has been collecting children's toys—brittle, cracked, damaged, cheap plastic toys—and leaves them on the floor near the garage door when he comes in. I move a broken truck from where it has been left to trip over and Dad immediately notices.

"Where is my truck?" he demands.

He says he is going to give these toys to someone, but of course a hoarder does not simply give things away. A hoarder only adds to their collection, each item bursting with the potential of a future use. This potential, which a hoarder seeks to conserve no matter the cost, only lasts as long as it is never realized. A hoarder keeps things because of the past, and because of the future.

I suggest to Dad that these toys were already discarded, that he took them out of people's garbage by the side of the road.

"Oh no," he says. "No one would have thrown these away. These are good toys."

His plastic truck has a big crack through its body. Yes, and all four wheels. The windshield is broken but can be fixed. Someone might want it.

I use the cracked truck as a bin to collect all Dad's toys in one place. He can see at a glance that his inventory is secure. Someone does want these damaged toys.

I would understand being upset seeing your handiwork torn apart and tossed away. My father installed the sink and the counter in the old laundry room, and helped build the cupboards beneath the sink and the drawers under the counter.

But what Dad complains about is the old toilet from the half bath next to the laundry room. When he saw that old toilet on the dump trailer Dad wanted it taken back off and saved. This was another dramatic scene I am not sorry to have missed.

"It was perfectly good," he tells me. "We could have used that toilet in the new bathroom instead of buying a new one."

"The new toilet is better," I say. "It's low flow, and the seat is much higher."

I refrain from emphasizing that the decision to install a raised toilet was made for the benefit of my ninety-one-year-old father. The spacious new main-floor bathroom replacing the laundry room is also intended to help Dad "age in place."

"We didn't need a new toilet," Dad says. "There was nothing wrong with the old one. It was low flow too, because I put bricks in the tank."

"It was stained, Dad."

We now have a better well, but for decades our water was loaded in iron. Untreated, the water was orange and rank. Even with a water softener and filters, stubborn rust stains built up in the toilets and the bathtub. When I visited, I learned not to pack light-coloured clothing for fear of rust stains in the wash. (I also never brought my favourite clothes or bright colours, because my mother treated colour in my clothes like a form of dirt demanding bleach.)

I used to come home, and before I had my first shower, crawl around in the bathtub and scrub hard for half an hour removing what I could of the rust stains. I did this for my mother. She'd burst into tears when she saw the tub temporarily almost stain free. It was her extreme gratitude that prompted me to assign myself this chore.

Dad is not ready to give up on the old stained toilet that has already gone to the dump. "It could be cleaned," he says.

"Were you going to clean it?" I ask, my voice rising to an accusatory pitch. "Have you ever cleaned a toilet and tried to remove rust stains? Even once in your life?"

———

I AM STANDING LOOKING OUT the living room window. The picture window frames a view of the seasonal pond, the greenhouse, the big garden, and the land to the river. Across the road from the garden is the new fire hall, now several years old but still called new.

"You have a gut now," Dad says. "Your belly really sticks out."

Even though new windows were installed months ago, there are still little piles of debris left here and there—bits of pink fibreglass insulation, sawdust, wooden shims and scraps. A couple of windows, the guts of their framing exposed, await inside finishing trim.

The curtain rods all came down and don't fit the new windows. I sweep up the mess in the dining room and wonder if I can adjust to life in a fishbowl, without drapes or blinds in any of the windows.

Dad suggests putting the old drapes back up. The living room drapes were a busy floral pattern, sun-rotted and hideous. The gaudy print clashed with everything in the room—I guess my mother enjoyed the clamour and the conversation. The truth is I always hated my mother's living room drapes and cannot imagine making the effort to find curtain rods to fit the new windows, only to then put up rotten old dirty drapes that I don't dare wash, because they would probably fall apart, and don't want to re-hang in the first place because I never could stand the sight of them.

I suppose I could try washing them, but I'd be very disappointed if they survived.

Sorry, Mom. I hated your tacky decor.

If I'm going to find drapes for all the windows they will have to be something I like. I throw the best of what we have in the washer, and repurpose the survivors for the den and bedrooms. Then I go shopping. For greater freedom, I will pay for everything. Dad's attitude is that the old drapes are fine and doesn't want to waste money replacing them. I'm not going to spend my father's money on a project he does not endorse.

"Just put up the old ones," he tells me again, when I talk to him about options.

I try to justify my decision. "I have to find new curtain rods. I can't find the same kind of curtain rods for that old style of drapes. People don't seem to use curtain hooks anymore."

The fact is, I know nothing about drapes and curtain rods or interior decorating. I go shopping, look around, come back to the family home, and stare at myself reflected in the naked windows. At the end of the day, life in a fishbowl means seeing yourself everywhere, staring into your own startled reflection, while around you the world outside is sensed, but cannot easily be seen.

"Dad, do you have any sort of preference for living room drapes?"

"Yes," he says.

"Okay," I say, knowing from his impish twinkle what he is going to say.

"I prefer the old ones."

"Do you know where I can get curtain rods to fit the old ones?"

"Use the old curtain rods."

"Dad, I told you. The old curtain rods are too short for the new windows."

"Oh," he says. He's just needling me, but luckily (as I keep reminding myself) my well of patience is infinite.

"So, you don't have any kind of preference for drapes for the living room?"

"I guess not," he says.

After visiting every store between Greenwood and New Minas, I find something suitable. The curtain rods are from Home Depot, and the drapes, from Zellers, have the appearance of rich brown silk, with a subtle golden sheen.

My brother installs the new curtain rods in the living room, while I pretend to help. In no time, new faux silk drapes are doing their quiet best to transform the tired space. I'm actually quite proud of myself. The effect is simple and masculine, and the colours hum a quiet harmony, rather than everything in the room yelling at each other.

I step farther back to admire the rich sheen of the new drapes from another angle. "How do you like that, Dad?"

He glances up from his sudoku. "I don't like brown curtains," he says.

My pride deflates. This project consumed hours of time and a few hundred dollars. I think the curtains look great, but it is my father's house. I was trying to make him happy.

"Well," I manage to say, without being the least bit snippy, "you might have said that when I asked if you had any preferences."

"There's nothing you can do to make him happy," my brother says. "He's just so hateful."

The plumber hired to work in the house tells my brother he wants to quit. My father's constant bossy nagging and criticism is an ordeal.

"He's only been here a few days," I scoff. "Try growing up with it."

Renovation options are discussed with Dad, but then he claims no one said anything to him.

"Where's the washer and dryer going to be?" he asks.

"In the garage," I say.

"First I've heard of it," he claims, thumping the arm of his chair with the heel of his hand.

For the first couple of days I didn't know what the hell was going on, but now I make sure Dad and I have discussed everything he claims no one has told him about. Renovations are always a challenge—now imagine the homeowner forgets the plan they agreed to from one day to the next.

One of the plumber's assistants is banging on pipes in the basement and Dad looks up from his puzzle. "What the dickens?"

Dad bustles down to the basement to investigate. I follow him and stand in the garage near the basement stairs to listen. The plumber is already upset about the amount of time being wasted on this project.

When we first moved into this house it was still under construction, so the washing machine was—temporarily—installed in the basement. I guess this was Dad's idea, because it was certainly the most inconvenient spot to put it. It meant a whole lot of stairs for whoever actually used the washing machine. My mother complained bitterly about the need to haul dirty laundry all the way down to the cold basement, and then lug heavy wet clothes back up two flights of stairs to hang out on the line. (The dryer was not installed at all until the laundry room was finished. And finishing the laundry room took a lot of nagging.)

The plumber's assistant is preparing to run waterlines into the garage from the basement, working in the same spot where the washing machine was inconveniently located all those years ago. The hookup for the washing machine is still in place.

"What are you doing?" Dad asks.

"I'm going to tap these pipes and run water over there for the washer."

"There's no need to do that." Dad indicates the hot and cold taps. "Everything you need is right here."

"I thought the washer was going in the garage, next to the stairs."

"No," Dad says. "It's going right here."

"What about the utility sink?" asks the assistant. "Is it still going in the garage?"

I decide to intervene. "Everything's going in the garage," I say. I step down onto the basement stairs and bend over so I can see Dad and the plumber. "The sink, the washer, and the dryer are all going in the garage. It's more convenient there."

Dad inhales sharply to puff himself up and turns to me. "Go upstairs and be quiet," he snaps.

I back away towards the garage door and wait while Dad climbs the stairs from the basement and then up from the garage to the main floor. His angry slippers scuff overhead, heading back to his chair.

"Sorry," I say to the young assistant plumber. "He gets confused sometimes."

"Don't I know you?" he says. "You're in my crossbow club."

"No," I say, a little flustered. "That's not me."

Workers come and go and it is an eye-opener to see how they treat my father. Some are kind and perfectly polite, but others do not acknowledge Dad exists. Clearly, in their eyes he is just an ancient old man in a chair. And therefore, irrelevant.

The rude ones don't even say hello to him. As they pass the living room, they greet me and ask me questions as if I am the one in charge. Good manners dictate they at least say hello to Dad in his own home.

It will now be apparent to even the most forgiving reader that I am an outrageous hypocrite. I'd be the first to admit that my father's not really in charge of these renovations, yet I expect tradesmen, practical types paid by the hour, to act a little more duplicitous towards him. In effect what I want to say is this: *Why don't you humour him, like I do? Why don't you just let him ramble, and pretend to be interested in what he might have to say?*

I want the workers to chat with Dad, to flatter him, and to manage him—if only to make my short visit more peaceful.

Is that really too much to expect?

I want them to at least say hello when they enter his house.

I can see he is offended when he is completely ignored, and simmers with resentment when someone directs a question to me instead of asking him. Being ignored like that is strong evidence of creeping irrelevance, and I suspect Dad all too clearly grasps exactly what is happening.

Although he could never articulate it.

So maybe Dad fumed over the rudeness of some workers, and out of that slow burn came his suspicions. He doesn't accuse anyone in particular, but he tells me that the workers are stealing his popcorn.

Oh Jesus, no. Not the popcorn again.

Dad's popcorn used to be one of his obsessions. He grew it—popcorn is just a special type of corn that, if dried correctly, will explode when heated. Dad found popcorn "seed corn" in a seed catalogue and figured we'd never have to buy popcorn again.

Dad's seeds produced small short cobs with pointy little rounded kernels shaped like tiny hanging drops. These tiny kernels did not look anything like popcorn from the store. He bought a special popcorn popper for the microwave and insisted, again and again, on popping his own corn. Even if the little kernels popped—many of them simply refused—they rarely achieved the lack of tooth-jolting hardness that one looks for in a handful of munchable popcorn. Here's a fun fact—popped kernels of Dad's corn were often no bigger and only slightly less hard than unpopped kernels from the store.

In other words, Orville Redenbacher didn't need to worry about competition from my father.

Dad kept planting this uninviting popcorn, fussing over the crop, and popping up batch after batch that no one wanted to pick through and attempt to eat. Dad never admitted that his popcorn was anything less than a success. No one else would bother to initiate this, so Dad himself nuked batches in his special popper, and stubbornly munched away at his homegrown popcorn.

As a teenager I lived a wild, reckless life. In one of my most fear-less escapades, I even went so far as to dare to buy popcorn from the store. (I know—completely out of control.)

"Who bought this?" Dad demanded.

I admitted my guilt.

"What's wrong with the popcorn I grow?" he asked, as if it wasn't obvious.

I was never really that shy about detailing the many failings of Dad's pet popcorn. It was a treat, though, to be asked. Besides letting Dad know his popcorn was "too hard" and "basically inedible," I told him I got the store-bought kind because "I wanted real popcorn for a change."

Dad could not bear the thought of spending two dollars for a bag of popcorn that produced great heaping mounds of fluffy goodness, but had no difficulty with us all spending hours in the garden tending rows of popcorn plants that produced nothing but pointy little hard kernels. Even if these tiny kernels had been properly dried, they could never have produced anything but the sort of half-popped sad little specimens ignored at the bottom of the bowl after you've eaten all the puffy, tasty bits.

Dad grew his popcorn year after year, unwilling to give up on it, and there is still to this day a collection of unloved stubby little cobs gathering dust in the basement. They have been mouldering there in a cardboard flat for decades.

Some kernels are missing from the cobs, and Dad's theory is that the workers are stealing his popcorn.

Dad could not give this popcorn away to hungry teenagers but now imagines workers are stealing it. Who would even recognize these stubby cobs of pointy little kernels as being popcorn, much less want to steal some? Who steals a handful of dusty corn from a basement?

"It's more likely to be mice, Dad."

He refuses to believe that. "We don't have mice," he declares.

I set some traps but never do catch any mice.

Later, however, while cleaning up the basement and the rec room, I find little stashes of popcorn kernels in corners and in boxes sprinkled with mouse droppings. Dad's missing popcorn has been found.

Almost all of the popcorn is accounted for. The elusive mice might have hoarded it, but even they found the hard old kernels too unpleasant to actually eat.

3

DO YOU WANT TO
SEE MY P—N—S?

*Perseveration: In psychology, to continue or repeat an
activity or mental state to an unusual degree.*

IF YOU SHOULD HAPPEN TO LINGER in the parking lot of the store
next to my father's house, you might glance up to see Dad bent in
your direction, leaning heavily on his grey metal cane—if he has
remembered to use it. He will be wearing an old plaid shirt torn at the
elbow and frayed at the collar and cuffs. His jeans are faded, ripped,
and stained. He does not lace up his old workboots, so he can't really
pick up his feet and walk. His little steps are brisk and even but also a
bit frantic, like a windup toy headed towards the table's edge.

He shuffles directly towards you, perhaps interrupting your conversation. His teeth are loose, so his top plate clacks as he works it
with his tongue while making his beeline. A side effect of his blood

pressure medication is excessive saliva so there may be some drool when he starts talking, especially if he gets excited.

He's bent over, ancient, drooling, and dressed in stained rags. He scuffs up to you, dragging his feet, and says, "Do you want to see my pee-nuhss?"

Now, what would you do?

If a decrepit old man asked if you wanted to see his penis, would you phone the police? Because people did. People complained to the Royal Canadian Mounted Police about my father. According to the local paper's chatty police column, the RCMP responded to reports of an elderly man asking an inappropriate question in the parking lot of my brother's store. However, the police investigation never extended as far as actually talking to my father or his family.

You see, my father was already notorious. The police knew all about him. He's probably already shuffled up to them. If RCMP officers were to observe Dad approaching, they surely have learned to hop back into their cruiser and speed away to a safe space. Many people flee the parking lot of my brother's store when Dad is on patrol.

And that brings us to my next question: What would you do if an old man totters up and asks if you want to see his peanuts?

Imagine the word slurred through loose dentures and excessive drool. Imagine you are in Nova Scotia and not somewhere much warmer, like, say, Georgia. Imagine my father asking this question without any context or preliminaries. Imagine an old man so excited he has no time to enunciate.

No wonder people mishear.

Try saying "peanuts" aloud, and slur the consonants a bit. Emphasize the s at the end more than the t. Say peanuts without the t. Let's say it together: "pee-nuhss." Pretend a stranger approaches you in a parking lot, and he is eager to ask your children his pressing question. Pretend this stranger will not take no for an answer.

If you do say no, he counters with, "Why not?"

What would you do?

Would you gather up your children and take them to see what the old man wants to show off?

Because many people do.

My father's obsession with peanuts is seriously embarrassing—and a marvel of determination and focus.

This is a man who enjoys calls from telemarketers because he can talk to them about peanuts. If the phone rings and it is a wrong number, guess what? Through sheer strength of will Dad can grab on to any caller and force a conversation. It is strangely beautiful how he can seize the most unlikely opportunity.

If my father is trying to reel someone in and feeling diplomatic, he uses a two-step approach. First he asks, "Do you garden?"

The answer is of no concern. Yes, no, never—it does not matter. The first question is only the lead-in for the second: "Do you know what I grow?"

Now here, sometimes people do say "peanuts" because they have been down this road before. They've called the wrong number and talked to my father about peanuts. Dad asks many people many times because he just has to keep asking everybody because he does not want to risk overlooking a single person.

Most people cannot guess what my father grows. He says "Peanuts and sweet potatoes," or sometimes just, "Peanuts." He makes it sound like he is growing a big crop, and he did grow a good crop of sweet potatoes, more than we could eat or give away. But he does not get anything out of the peanuts. The few plants he grows are nothing but pets. In fact, Dad drags so many people into the garden to see his peanut plants the ground is packed down hard and it's a miracle if anything grows. At least all the traffic keeps the weeds down. In the unlikely event any peanuts are produced, they are kept for seed. We never ate a single peanut from a plant that he grew. Not once. Not a single peanut ever did we eat. I cannot emphasize this enough. The peanuts are just for show and tell.

I often ask Dad what it is about peanuts he find so compelling he cannot stop searching for new people to tell about them. I never get an answer that makes sense to me. As close as I can come to constructing an explanation is this: Around eighty years ago someone showed Dad how peanuts grew and this encounter was so (magnificent?), that it somehow percolated for the rest of his life? Dad wants other people to have the same opportunity to learn about peanuts. He does not want anyone to miss out. Do you understand now? It might be the only chance in their entire lifetime to see a peanut plant. It would be a real shame for them to miss it.

In his enthusiasm, it does not matter to Dad whether people are the slightest bit interested in peanuts. He will ask everybody, simply everybody, "Do you want to see my peanuts?" It is totally up to them what they hear in his innocent, hopeful question.

———

I TELL DAD HE DRESSES LIKE A HOMELESS PERSON, and he just laughs.

"Don't you have better clothes?" I ask.

"Yeah."

"Why don't you wear them?"

"What's wrong with what I have on?"

"Your shirt is torn and look at the stains on those jeans," I say.

"They're clean."

"How often are they washed?"

Dad claims his shirt is washed every week and his jeans every two weeks. I permit myself to be skeptical. Dad showers once a week, on Sunday. I have been here since Tuesday and he has worn the same clothes every day. By Friday, I was complaining about always seeing him in the same ratty clothes, and he said he would change on Sunday, when he has his shower.

"I don't smell," Dad says, but then falters. "Do I?"

"No, you don't," I admit.

My nose is keen, often much too keen, and yet Dad has no detectable aroma. As far as my nose is concerned, he's invisible. Now that he's mentioned it, his complete lack of odour is most peculiar. Most people smell of *something*.

Sunday morning, he comes downstairs after his shower dressed in the same old rags.

"Dad—*what* are you wearing?" *God, I sound just like my mother.*

"I'll change them next week."

"You said you would change them today."

I stand my ground. Yes, I intend to make my ninety-two-year-old mobility-impaired father climb back up the stairs to change his clothes.

"I'm sick of looking at those old things," I say. "Do you need new clothes? Let's go up and see what you have. Yes, I'm serious. Go back up there and change your clothes like you said you were going to."

I'm definitely channelling Mom.

The few clothes Dad normally wears are piled on a chair in his bedroom. In his musty closet I discover a very nice cotton shirt, thick and fleecy. "Why don't you wear this good shirt? It looks warm."

"Can't," he says. "I've only got one."

"What do you mean?"

"When I change out of it, it will be too much of a shock. I changed shirts once when I was six and got a terrific cold."

I take a deep breath. Is this why he wears the same thing every day—because he is afraid to shock his system? Or has he just announced another inconsistent policy—that he will only wear something if he has two of the same thing? Good to know, since we are going shopping, but I have to roll my eyes. Dad complains of feeling a chill but will not wear his nice warm shirt because he caught cold eighty-six years ago.

Complaining is one of my father's last comforts, and he will not be prodded into giving it up for good. He'd rather complain than change.

Dad's ratty old plaid shirt goes into the wash and then mysteriously disappears—another trick learned from Mom. His threadbare old jeans are no less stained when they come out of the laundry. Dad claims they are his warmest jeans, but what fabric remains is about as thin and supple as a T-shirt.

Dad says, "The stains make them warmer." He thinks that's funny. He squeezes a good laugh out of his joke.

I enjoy the moment, and that is what it is. A moment. The big picture is full of moments.

———

I PLAN A SHOPPING TRIP WITH DAD to Greenwood. We'll get him some jeans and then go to the health food store that he likes across from the mall.

When we arrive at Mark's, Dad hands me his cane and furniture surfs over to men's wear. He quickly messes up the neat piles of jeans. He is wielding a tape measure; the stiff yellow tongue juts out, tasting and rejecting one pair after another. The tape measure is not a good sign.

A young female clerk offers to help. "What size are you looking for?"

"Eleven inches," he says.

"Is it for a child?"

"No," Dad says. "For me."

"What size are you?" she asks.

"Eleven inches," he says again. "I need an eleven-inch zipper."

The clerk glances at me. She looks like a high school student, but might be in her young twenties. If I could, I would shrink into something much smaller than eleven inches and disappear entirely from view.

"What we have is here," she says, indicating the array of men's jeans. "Let me know if you need any help."

She gives me what I interpret as a sympathetic look, conveying with a glance that I am to take over.

The search for an eleven-inch zipper is a very recent quest for my father, and one that is impervious to reason. Perhaps he had such trousers back in the 1930s when high waists were the style and he was as slender as a reed. Certainly his current jeans, and the ones he has worn for decades, have no such feature. He might be able to find pants with eleven-inch zippers at some funky vintage place. Or he could have his pants custom made. I have explained all this to him.

I had no idea he was going to pull out a retractable metal tape measure in Mark's Work Wearhouse and declare his need for an eleven-inch zipper.

He gives up on finding proper jeans. What he really wants is long underwear, the thermal tops and bottoms that he sleeps in. He's very particular about his long underwear.

"You know what killed your grandfather, don't you?" Dad says. "He went to the hospital and they took him out of his long underwear."

That sequence of events is more or less true (Dad's father went to the hospital, and then into an old-age home, and then he died), but there were many reasons why my eighty-five-year-old grandfather was admitted to hospital. Removing Grampy's long underwear was never confirmed as the official cause of death, but for years Dad has been recollecting what he considers to be his father's final fatal misstep. Perhaps the point of the story is that, when the time comes, we are to insist that our father remains clad in his life-preserving long johns.

At the checkout Dad is shocked by the price of his thermal layers, even though he paid the same price last year for the same brand at the same store. He acted shocked last year too. It is something he does every time he buys anything. His mouth hangs open and he looks around as if he has just been asked to fly to the moon. Then he shakes his head and sighs.

He intends to pay by cheque but does not even start looking for his chequebook until he has gone all the way through his performance of shock at the price. Paying by cheque is a slow process, and Dad's cramped handwriting has only one concentrated speed. This single shopping trip with my father is enough to make it obvious why stores no longer accept cheques. Life is just too short.

The lineup behind us at the cash register is growing.

The cashier, another young woman, is exceedingly kind and patient with my father. He keeps asking what the amount is, because he cannot remember—or refuses to believe it. The cashier writes the total on a piece of paper and slides it across the counter so Dad has it right in front of him.

When he hands her the cheque, he asks, "Do you garden?"

I want to crawl into my own little hole and die. I glance behind us at the line of impatient shoppers. There are some dirty looks.

"We need to go, Dad," I say.

"Hush now," he snaps at me, and switches to a pleasant tone to address the kind and patient cashier. "Guess what I grow."

"Not now, Dad. There's people waiting."

He turns to me with a swell of anger: "Will you be quiet!" Then back to the cashier: "Peanuts," he says in a rush. "I grow peanuts."

(At least, "peanuts" is what Dad means to say.)

"Really," she says. "Wow."

Dad storms off away from me in a huff, as much as is possible for a ninety-two-year-old who shuffles little baby steps. When he gets like this, it is his elbows that give him away—in their flare and space-taking. His arms swing out wide behind him as he totters off, elbows cocked at angry angles.

I gather up the purchases Dad left on the counter and catch the kind cashier's eye. "Sorry," I say.

"It's okay," she says. "We all have parents."

In his huff, Dad scurries right past the store exit and is stuck at the entrance, unable to pass the wrong way through the turnstiles. He tries each one, but none will let him out.

"What is going on?" he says. "Isn't this where we came in?"

"Yes," I say, "but the exit is over there."

"What next." He has starting saying "what next" a lot, and not as a question.

Frustrated now by the confusing layout of the store, he seems to have forgotten—or is willing to overlook—my incredible rudeness.

At the health food store the owner knows Dad by name. On each visit he spends two or three hundred dollars on vitamins, treats such as yogurt-covered raisins that are essentially candy, and food such as Black Mission figs, apricots, and, yes, the thick rich nutritious nectar of the gods—organic peanut butter.

"Now what do I need?" he asks the owner.

"I don't know, Stephen. Did you bring a list?"

"Oh yes. The list."

Dad brings out his little notebook. Indeed he does have a list of things he needs at the health food store. In fact, he has several very similar lists of things he needed at the health food store, none of them dated. Dad flips back and forth in his notebook, muttering quietly. The procedure to determine which shopping list might be for today is not quick.

Eventually, he decides on a list and reads from his little notebook. The store owner selects the items. She seems to know more about what Dad wants than he does. His list says "Vit C," but he does not know what format or dosage. The owner fills in the blanks.

My father has trouble making out his own handwriting. I'm trying to read over his shoulder. I reach out to tilt his notebook a little towards me, but he jerks it away and moves so I can't see it anymore. Finally, he offers his notebook to the store owner, and she is able to decipher his scrawl.

When we get home I tell my brother I'm never taking Dad shopping again.

"Told you," he says.

———

AFTER THIS EXPEDITION deep into my wide-open shame zone I try to understand why being in public with my father is so mortifying. Other people find Dad sweet and amusing, but I rarely do anymore, and not just because he's rude with his family. The cashier was kind and patient—where is my kindness, my patience?

Where is my infinite well of patience? It starts out well, but then, well, converts in a flash to a bitter well.

Everything my father does feels like a reflection of me. A reflection from hidden depths.

As soon as I spend time with my father, my boundaries suddenly revert to being fluid, and completely porous. I suppose it was like that with my mother, too, but it's been so long I can't really remember the feeling. My father, though, is still here, still in my face and in my body, and in my own bumbling long-distance manner, I'm trying to help him—whether he wants it or not.

I used to go home for a week or so, every few years. Now I've started going twice a year, for as long as three weeks at a time. Spending so much time with my father—five or six weeks a year—means I need to deal with all the stuff that keeps coming up. All my stuff, buried deep and festering.

My experience shopping with my father triggers deep layers of shame and so many memories of bullying and public ridicule.

When you are a teenager, your parents exist only as obstructions and as embarrassments.

My grade ten biology teacher lived in Berwick and commuted to West Kings District High School, driving an old hearse. It was decommissioned, no longer black. Basically this vehicle presented as a long green station wagon, extra roomy in back.

"Decommissioned" is a very particular word. No one says decommissioned bread truck, or decommissioned school bus, but if people knew one thing about "Gruesome Gorman" it was that he commuted to school in his old hearse. A *decommissioned* hearse.

I had no warning what was about to happen that morning in biology. Mr Gorman said, "We have a special guest," and in walked my father, brandishing a handful of his fucking peanut plants.

Dad saw me at breakfast. Like an hour ago. He couldn't mention he was coming to my class?

Dad has a little routine he does, explaining the natural wonders of the majestic peanut plant. It is perhaps an interesting little routine, if you have never heard it before, and if you gave even the smallest single fuck about peanuts.

However, his presentation on the magic of peanuts lasted no longer than one minute. Ninety seconds tops. After that, it was time for questions. There were none. Mr Gorman made a couple of comments in the form of questions, which prompted my father to repeat what he had already said (the peanut blossoms above the ground, and then each flower stem goes down into the dirt and that's where the peanuts grow. Yes. Underground. Yes, in the dirt).

And that's more or less it.

I was embarrassed beyond my ability to feel any more ashamed. My status at school was already rock bottom, so I tried to console myself believing that my father's peanut presentation was unlikely to make my situation any worse. In fact, by the end of class I doubt any of my bored/stoned/sleepy classmates even remembered this brief and bizarre early-morning peanut interlude. It's perfect being so beneath contempt people don't even bother gathering ammunition against you.

My classmates may not have given it a second thought, but I hold on to this memory for the rest of my life. My father's peanut presentation to my grade ten science class was underwhelming yet totally mortifying.

All of high school in a nutshell.

(And just to be clear—that is not a pun. A peanut is not a nut. It is a legume. Peanuts do not grow on trees. They grow underground. Please pay attention.)

———

DAD'S SISTER, MAXINE, IS IN THE HOSPITAL. Maxine asked someone to call Dad to let him know she is in Valley Regional.

Aunt Maxine and Uncle Ken are both around Dad's age and live in Wolfville, about twenty miles away. Dad does not see them very often. And by not often, I mean not for years. Ken and Maxine used to occasionally drive out to see Dad, but Maxine frowned upon the state of Dad's home. The living room, for example, was so cluttered with piles of dusty junk three people could not all sit down at the same time. On their last trip Maxine refused to even go inside. She rolled down her car window and talked to Dad as he stood in the driveway next to their car. Maxine then found my brother and complained to him.

"It's disgusting," she said. "I'm not coming back unless you do something."

"All the more reason never to clean," my brother said.

So, the last time Dad saw his sister was years ago, and he only talked to her in the driveway.

Dad has the phone volume cranked up so high I can easily eavesdrop on his calls from across the room, but I don't let on.

"Who was that, Dad?"

"Maxine is in the hospital." Dad sets down the phone.

"Do you want to go visit her?"

"Don't know if she wants me to," he says.

"Do you want to see her?" I ask again. "I'll drive you."

"She might not want visitors," he says.

"Dad, I'm asking what you want to do."

He just looks at me, and then returns to his sudoku. I've hit his wall. He cannot, or will not, say what he wants.

"Okay, Dad, this is how I see it. Maxine is in the hospital. She had someone call you to let you know, because she does want to see you. She probably wants to say goodbye. This might be the last chance to see her before she dies. Now—what do you think? Should we go see her?"

I can't recall the last time I spoke to my father so clearly and directly about an important emotional issue. I spell it all out, everything that was incredibly obvious, and he watches me silently, his stubby pencil poised over his smudged puzzle. I even remember to ask what he thinks, not what he feels, in the hope of getting a response.

"Okay," Dad says. "We can go."

If I hadn't been sitting right there when that call came in, eavesdropping shamelessly, Dad would have hung up the phone and simply forgot all about his sister in the hospital.

The last time I saw my aunt Maxine was when my mother died. Maxine thought the reception line in the Anglican Church Hall following my mother's funeral service was the ideal place to pepper me with questions about what I was doing with my life. At the time, I was basically unemployed and living in Montreal, pretending to be a writer, so perhaps I was primed to feel a mite defensive.

I tried to deflect Maxine's probing with vague answers and platitudes, expecting she would move along. She ignored my weak murmurs. She demanded to know exactly what my plans were, and when I was going to start getting serious. She thought I was going to be a lawyer—what happened to that?

Maxine's voice was whiny and nasal, and she came across as judgmental more than caring. My mother had just been killed, suddenly, tragically, in a car accident—surely I couldn't be expected to tolerate career questions at her funeral.

For whatever reason, Maxine felt like being pushy and obnoxious. Well guess what? We're related. Sometimes bitchy, nagging spouses become used to their silent partners—beleaguered peacemakers who prefer not to engage. But I am not like that. I have words and know how to use them. I can push back if provoked.

"Look, Maxine," I said, not even bothering to speak quietly. "You've never shown any interest in my life before, and I hardly think this is the time, or the place, for you to start." My dead mother, my trump card, hovered in the air next to me. Mom despised Maxine.

Uncle Ken was British and extremely embarrassed. He had been tugging on Maxine's arm for much of her interrogation, trying to move her along away from me, and finally succeeded.

It has never crossed my mind in the last twenty-odd years to go see Maxine while visiting Nova Scotia. Oh sure, I've offered to take Dad to Wolfville anytime he wanted, but the idea of visiting his sister never seemed to cross his mind either.

And now here we are, heading down Brooklyn Street, the back way to Valley Regional, going to see Maxine in the hospital.

This is the route that Dad prefers. He provides directions at every turn, as if I haven't been driving these exact same roads since I was a teenager.

Maxine is in what is euphemistically called a semi-private room. Her bed is next to the window. Ken is seated in a chair at the foot of the bed. He stands when we come in. Ken is friendly and greets me warmly. I say hello to Maxine, who is unable to talk easily, and chat with Ken. He is in his nineties, and very sweet. When he dies, we discover he survived torpedo attacks on three different ships during his wartime service in the merchant marine. We didn't know—he never happened to mention it. In fact, I am dumbfounded to realize that I do not recall ever speaking to him in my life, except on this day at the foot of Aunt Maxine's hospital bed.

Dad does not greet his sister or his brother-in-law. He has not made it past the other bed in the room, the one closer to the door. He strikes up a conversation with the very weak woman in that bed and with her visitor. He wants to know if they garden. The weak woman, who is not that old but shrunken and withered by the illness draining her, confesses that she has, without much success, tried to grow herbs in a window box.

"Guess what I grow," Dad says, excited by his catch.

I stand next to Uncle Ken and watch this spectacle, as if from afar. Dad's peanut obsession is in full bloom. He wants to arrange to show his peanuts to this patient in the palliative care ward. He launches into detailed directions.

"It's the first house on the right as you come off the highway," Dad says. "Or will you be taking the old number one?"

This woman, thin and drawn, looks like she has difficulty navigating to the bathroom without assistance and Dad imagines she might drive out to Berwick to see his peanuts. He repeats the directions, two or three times, just to make sure she understands.

"I'm serious," he says. "Come by anytime."

Only after he has cleared the path of all peanut novices is Dad free to continue towards the bed that holds his one and only sister.

In his heavy old untied workboots, Dad clomps and scuffs over to his sister's bedside. They try to talk, but Maxine is weak and has difficulty breathing, so she can only whisper. Dad refuses to wear his expensive hearing aids, so I have to insert myself right in the middle of what could have been their tender scene and repeat every soft thing Maxine says much louder directly at Dad.

She thanks him for coming to see her.

"What?" Dad says, turning to me.

"THANK YOU FOR COMING."

"You were always a good brother to me," she whispers.

"You were a good brother."

"Huh?" Dad says.

"YOU WERE ALWAYS A GOOD BROTHER."

"I remember the watch you gave me when I went to nursing school."

"SHE REMEMBERS THE WATCH YOU GAVE HER."

"When I went to nursing school," she repeats. "My first watch."

"THE WATCH YOU GAVE HER WHEN SHE WENT TO NURSING SCHOOL. IT WAS HER FIRST WATCH."

"Uh-huh," Dad says.

"So thoughtful," Maxine says, using very little breath to talk. "Such a good brother."

I repeat her words, loudly, right at Dad. And then there is a lull.

The lull yawns wider.

I nudge my father. "Is there anything you'd like to say?"

"No," he says quickly, not even bothering to really think about it. A quick little aspirated "No," formed on the inhale.

Wow, I think, *that is my father on full display. Unbelievable.*

Dad in one economical syllable: "No."

I don't think he even said hello to Ken, whom Dad has known for more than sixty years.

It's not just me who Dad freezes out. It's not just me who seems to rank far down on his list of priorities.

Dad enters his sister's hospital room and immediately demonstrates that indulging his peanut obsession is far more important than family. He has hundreds of words for a stranger and only one for his sister.

When it was his chance to speak, to say goodbye to his sister, he froze. He didn't even bother to try. He didn't say a frigging thing, except his casual inhaled "No." He had a whole day to plan for this visit—was it so hard to find a few words to say to someone he grew up with and has known for ninety years?

Not that long ago, Dad hopped on a bus and went to Kentville by himself and spent $6,000 on hearing aids. He went in with a discount coupon for something basic, but a smarmy, flirtatious sales rep got her painted claws into him, and he was charmed into shelling out for a much fancier model that he will, supposedly, "grow into."

These hearing aids are a whole other story that I won't get into right now. But don't you think he could have worn his expensive hearing aids when going to see his sister on her deathbed, just so he could talk with her, one last time? What else were the damn things for, except for quiet, irreplaceable moments like this? He does not need them for watching television—for his polka party and cowboy gospel music he just cranks up the volume to a thumping thirteen.

Being in a room with three relatives in their nineties was for me a rare privilege. I offer to take Dad to the hospital again to visit Maxine, anytime he wants.

He says, "I don't know if she's still there."

"It's easy to check, if you want to go."

Apparently, he does not want to go. My suggestion withers on the vine, unpicked, untouched.

He will never see his sister again.

In a few months, my brother and my father will go to Maxine's funeral. That is the last time they see Ken. Only later, reading Ken's obituary, will we learn about the torpedoes.

———

HERE'S SOMETHING I KEEP DISCOVERING. The closer I watch my father, the more I learn about myself. Deflecting Maxine's questions, at first with vagueness and then with aggression—where do you suppose I learned to do that? Being cold and standoffish when it suits me—gosh, that seems familiar.

How much real choice do we have in life? Despite myself I am turning into my father, and maybe that's not any sort of bad thing. As time passes and I learn to make friends with myself, I recognize that more and more I am guided by his personality. I am either "Dad," or its equal and opposite reaction: the "not-Dad." Not-Dad is still, in essence, shaped by Dad—by his shadow, by his behaviour, by the space he takes up in my psyche.

What did I learn from him? Stubbornness. How to be stubborn and non-communicative. How to use distractions to avoid facing challenges. How to not give an inch out of spite. How a cat can open the heart and absorb all the affection in a family. How to be angry, and controlling, and a micromanager. How to think you know better than anyone else. How to be incredibly rude, and how to be incredibly sweet.

How to embrace your obsessions.

How to stubbornly survive.

Surviving—that's the good news. That's as good as it gets.

As Dad says, and as I have started saying, "I'm still here."

Every time I go to Nova Scotia, Dad asks me the same question. He asks if I have seen his peanuts.

"I thought you had," he says, "but I wanted to make sure. No harm in asking."

4

THE WAR OF THE WALKER

Denial: A defense mechanism to protect against the experience of an unbearable reality. Denial may serve to mask a deliberate tactic of impression-management, manipulation, or avoidance.

THE LAST TIME AN OCCUPATIONAL THERAPIST CAME to assess Dad for Veterans Affairs, she had him try out a walker on the driveway. He listened to what she had to say, and was polite enough, but was gently noncommittal in that rigid way of his.

He said, "Not now."

He said, "Maybe next year."

Next year has already come and gone.

My mission on this trip is to get a walker and convince Dad to use it. He refuses to see how his mobility is teetering on the edge of a cliff. His mobility is actually great, for his age—but that is a major qualification, given that he is ninety-three. He does not realize how close he is to losing what he has. He is one fall away from being in a wheelchair the rest of his life. He is moving less and less because he cannot walk unassisted, yet refuses assistance, except from the "girls."

The women who are Dad's caregivers are called girls. He calls them girls; they refer to each other as girls. Many are grandmothers, but I call them girls because that is the label they themselves use. It is how they talk, so it is how we all talk.

Every time he goes outside, Dad walks hanging on to a care worker, yet he does not recognize this as walking with assistance. He says he is walking fine, without any help.

Can he possibly imagine the girls are holding his hand for any reason other than to provide support? His lack of insight is a challenge to navigate. Still, I suppose the whole human race copes with limited amounts of insight. Only when others disagree with the extent of our insight is it labelled denial.

Meanwhile, Dad is getting weaker by the day because he is not getting enough exercise.

Just try to introduce Dad to his blind spots. He gets mad if you want to help him. He is supposed to be the boss in every situation, and that means he will not accept advice. Especially from the "boys"—his sons.

My brother and I have an arrangement. Because I live in Vancouver and only see Dad twice a year, I get to be the bad guy. It's just easier if Dad is mad at me instead of taking it out on my brother. My father and brother are already living on top of each other; there's no point throwing fuel on that fire.

The way I look at it, I've been punching Dad's buttons for more than fifty years. There's no reason to hold back now.

Dad has a prescription for a walker from his doctor, so Veterans Affairs will pay for it. It is just a matter of picking one out.

I arrange a trip to the drugstore with Dad and Kim, his main caregiver. We don't tell Dad the purpose of the trip, so he doesn't get all worked up and feel cornered.

The store has a few models in stock to try out. Well, I try them out. I'm walking with them, sitting on the seat, oohing and aahing about brakes and shopping baskets. There is one model that catches my eye. It has all the features, plus is easily folded for transport. Sleek and simple. Four large wheels. Its reminds me of those sturdy-looking baby strollers that appear to be designed for rugged terrain.

Kim and the drugstore cashier encourage Dad to try it out. I step back. If I push, he will resist. Women can get away with stroking Dad's ego in a way that is blatantly manipulative. He thrives under the attention of women—he just laps it up.

He takes a few tentative steps with the walker. Kim and the cashier erupt with praise and encouragement: "Oh, Stephen, you look so good." "Wow, look at you go."

There is a look on my father's face—a flash of mischief.

Suddenly, he takes off. Before anyone can realize what is happening Dad is running—actually running—down the aisle in Larry's Pharmacy.

"Careful now," Kim says. "Don't be a show-off, Stephen." But she's laughing behind her hand. We are all incredulous. It is even hard for me to believe although I saw it myself.

We try not to let Dad see that we are laughing at the sight of him flying down the aisle—sprinting or loping so fast and then it is over. Did he use the brakes on the walker to slow himself down before crashing? Several big scampering strides and he was done. But perhaps this incredible display just shows how much Dad's mobility could improve with the merest touch of added stability. Who knew my father could scamper so fast?

I can't remember the last time I saw my father run. He never ran. I've always seen him as old—when I was born he was forty and recovering from major surgery. He regained his strength and was a hard worker, but men of his generation never ran. Now I have seen my father at age ninety-three take off and almost fly, anchored to the ground only by his grip on the handles of a miraculous walker.

Dad is too tall for the model in stock. A larger size is ordered in a process where we all pretend Dad wants this walker. I stand behind Dad, nodding my head, overriding his waffling. We all ignore his disinterest and lack of commitment.

And that's it. The walker is one week away from entering the field of battle.

———

ONE OF DAD'S CAREGIVERS suffers a devastating loss. Her husband is burning garbage in a barrel, a gust of wind lifts some papers and blows them under the woodshed next to their small house, and in no more than fifteen minutes their home is totally engulfed and goes up in flames. Cathy is lucky to have gotten out uninjured.

A benefit dance is held at the Berwick Fire Hall. Even though the new fire hall is right across the street from my father's house, Dad hasn't been there in years. But he goes to Cathy's fundraiser.

Dad has the chance to actually dance with real women at this event, so he is beaming. At one point, Dad dances with Cathy's sister.

Afterwards, Cathy's sister has a strange look on her face.

"What's wrong?" Cathy asks.

"I can't believe he did that," her sister says. "Old Mr Ilsley invited me over to his house. He said he wants to show me his, you know—his thing."

"His peanuts," Cathy says, laughing.

"What?"

"His peanuts! He grows peanuts!"

Dad cackles with pure joy when I tell him what Cathy's sister thought he said. He thumps the arm of his chair, his face gleeful and gleaming. He also finds it hilarious that people have reported him to the police.

"What next," he says, cackling afresh and shaking his head at the absurd world.

I marvel at his complete lack of shame.

It's not normal.

A lack of crippling shame is just not normal.

Dad's new walker arrives and I bring it into the house, right upstairs and into the living room.

Dad is seated in his lift chair. He scowls at me, and especially at the walker.

"What's with the face?"

"What's that thing for?"

"It's yours."

"It's not mine," Dad says. "I've never seen it before."

"You picked it out."

He claims to have no memory of trying it out. He scoffs at the notion he was running with it—the very idea is ridiculous.

My father's face sets against the sight of this monstrosity in his house.

I pretend this walker is the most exciting new toy I've had my mitts on in years. I practise going all around the main floor. I move the chesterfield a little bit to widen the path past the brick fireplace, and shove the cumbersome portable dishwasher over tighter against the killer microwave. I'm clearing the road of obstacles so Dad can do laps in the house all winter.

Several times, I show Dad the features ("Look. Brakes!") and demonstrate how fun and easy it is to walk with this, um, walker. The girls and I try to come up with a different name for the thing, since Dad is dead set against the word "walker." I suggest calling it the "shopping cart" because there is a basket attached, and Dad enjoys shopping for groceries. At the store Dad basically uses a shopping cart as a walker. He loves pushing the cart around the store, yet refuses to make the connection between how well he walks with it and the fact he is relying on the cart for stability. He insists he is just pushing the cart, not leaning on it. I agree the shopping cart is not holding him up—but adds just the touch of stability he needs. I try to sell the new thing (his "personal shopping cart") as a safety device, to prevent falls.

"I know you don't need it to walk, Dad. But it's there if you want to sit down. And it might prevent a fall."

A fall is the biggest danger Dad faces. A fall could easily mean the end of the world as we know it.

And he has already fallen several times. But he doesn't remember, so as far as he is concerned none of it ever happened.

It is hard to break through such a solid wall of total denial.

But what can you do? Lock him up in a box so he can never hurt himself?

An OT, an occupational therapist, is a specialist in mobility, safety, and function. When you spend any time around OTs you start thinking in terms of ADLs—activities of daily living, such as dressing, toileting, or cutting your own toenails. Many of us take these things for granted, but as soon as there is any sort of decline or impairment, the ADLs—and how to make them easier, or even possible—become the new focus of your life.

That is, if you have the right attitude.

If your attitude is one of denial, all the advice in the world just runs up against the stainless-steel wall that will not indulge the rust of reality.

One of my father's daily activities is preparing his own breakfast. Of course, first of all he has his wheatgrass juice, a portion of which he has taken out of the freezer the night before. After the wheatgrass juice he waits thirty minutes, then tucks into his morning carb fest: cereal and milk, as well as prunes and bran muffins, bread and peanut butter or jam. Dad has always loved his food.

Loves his food and is obsessed with being constipated, which explains why he eats so many prunes and bran muffins. Whether he is in fact "backed up," or instead, his bowels are much too loose from a daily overdose of explosive fibre, is a matter requiring investigation. Let's leave it at that. Let's just acknowledge we all spend an inordinate amount of time respecting my father's concerns surrounding the condition of his bowels. Let's just say this appears to be another instance of my father being an unreliable historian. Dad will claim he has not had a "movement" in three days, but the people who clean his toilet can confirm that truth is indeed a messy business.

Preparing such a hearty breakfast presents a challenge. Dad takes something from the fridge, turns with that one thing in his hand, and staggers across the kitchen. Between the fridge and the counter are several steps with nothing to hang on to. Turning and walking is a problem for Dad, because his head and body start to go before his feet get the message to move. Changing directions is particularly dangerous. Dad often loses his balance in these transitions and does frantic little staggering half steps to recover. He does not acknowledge that we started buying one-litre milk containers because the two-litre size, when full, is too heavy for him to lift out of the fridge, hold in his hands, turn, and carry to the counter.

There are so many changes that he never acknowledges, but please—don't get me started.

I show Dad how he can use his new "shopping cart" to make breakfast easier. You wheel the "shopping cart" to the fridge, load up the basket with milk and bread and jam and everything you need, and then wheel the "shopping cart" over to the table. All in one trip! It's a miracle!

Dad gives me one of those looks that would stop the uninitiated in their tracks. It's not fire you see but a cold wall. I'm immune to his steely glint because I've been fully inoculated—and I'm as stubborn as hell. I'm as stubborn as he is. I am not giving up on this mission. This is the war of the walker, and it is not over yet.

Not by a long shot.

It's just a matter of winning the war before the king is lost.

The walker remains in the living room. Sometimes the girls sit the laundry basket on it as they sort and fold.

Dad never touches it.

———

DAD REPEATEDLY TELLS ME A STORY about my brother. Ever since my brother renovated part of the house and attempted to clean up the garage, Dad's anger has been festering. As Dad's circle has shrunk, he lashes out where he can still reach. He kicks whatever is closest. Right now, his frustrations are directed towards my brother.

My brother became rebellious when he was fifteen, Dad tells me, and "I couldn't do anything with him anymore." Dad wanted "to do something, but your mother wouldn't let me."

Dad says, "It got so bad I had to give up on him."

This story is on his mind and he keeps dishing it up to me. I try to offer a different perspective and explain how normal it is for a teenager to rebel. Dad's position does not soften. My brother and my father are not getting along, and that colours Dad's view. But the simple truth is—they are too much alike. Everyone sees this but them. Tellingly, their inability to see how much they are alike is another way in which they are exactly alike.

Dad keeps reaching for this story of my brother's teenage rebellion because he wants to frame the narrative. Dad is trying, subconsciously, to find the foundation for the current discord.

It is extraordinary to me that Dad can tell this story, of giving up on his eldest son, without any awareness of the bad light his own account casts on him, as a parent. Every parent encounters rebellion, but how many think it justifies giving up?

And further to that, my brother was a model son—certainly a model I could never live up to. Out of one hundred teenagers, where zero is completely out of control, my brother was at least a ninety-five. I was no more than a seventy-five (and since I'm scoring myself, it is fair to impute a degree of prejudice). My brother was only the tiniest bit rebellious, but that was not true of me. To be completely fair, my bad influence dragged my brother's score down.

The next time Dad launches into how he "was forced to give up on your brother when he was fifteen," I have finally had enough.

I interrupt him with a question.

"How old was I when you gave up on me?"

He pauses midstream, then says, "Huh?"

I repeat my question, slowly, struggling to keep anger out of my voice. "How old. Was I. When. You. Gave up. On. Me?"

We don't talk for a while after this. Sometimes it seems that Dad does not remember our frank little exchanges, but I have to say, I never hear this story about my brother again.

I seize the opportunity to needle my brother about the change in fortunes. "I'm the favourite son now," I gloat. "I knew it would happen!"

Dad not only makes himself look bad with his version of events but also manages to blame our dead mother for preventing him from being a good parent. I am curious what measures Dad might have deployed to rein in a rebellious teenager. Beating your children was traditional in our family, but how well did that really work?

Being beaten pounded my budding defiance deeper into my bones, stiffening my resolve. And then, under the right conditions, my battle-hardened defiance would suddenly manifest.

There is one story I have recounted several times, mostly to therapists.

My story has various titles, including "The Legend of the Rake."

It was a warm summer's evening. I was probably thirteen or fourteen. I had just spent hours mowing the lawn, as I did every week. In damper places near the seasonal pond, where the grass grew fast and lush, the mower spewed out wet clumps in thick ragged chains. These areas had to be raked, or the lawn would die. And I would be in trouble.

Dad came by, told me to stop what I was doing and go work in the garden.

I said, "I have to finish this first."

He insisted I would do what I was told. I insisted I was going to finish this despised job before I started another one. And I went back to raking.

Dad grabbed the rake from me and started swinging at my legs with the handle. This was an old-fashioned lawn rake, with a sturdy wooden handle much thicker than a broomstick.

Dad was whacking me on the legs with the rake handle and I didn't even try to move away. I looked him right in the eye and said, "Beat me all you want—I'm not going to do it."

He became completely furious.

He clenched the rake tighter in his fists, knuckles whitening, and threatened the worst punishment he could imagine: "I'll take the TV away!"

I couldn't help myself—I laughed in his face.

That was his idea of escalation, threatening to take the television away? It seemed completely absurd. If beating me with the rake failed to persuade me, did he really think cutting off access to the TV would make me buckle? I loved watching television, sure, even though in good weather we had a grand total of two stations, and it would almost kill me not to watch *The Six Million Dollar Man*, which Dad thought was stupid. But he obviously did not know me very well. What was he going to do? Send me to my room, to read Dickens? As punishment?

If my father had been truly sophisticated in his desire to punish me, he would have taken away *Great Expectations*, separating me from my beloved Pip, and made me watch the television programs he enjoyed, like the down-home stylings of *Don Messer's Jubilee*. That truly would have been unendurable.

Luckily for me, such cruelty never crossed his mind.

Dad threw down the rake and stormed off, elbows flying in his wake, and that was it. That was a major moment in my early teens.

I had claimed my power. I was no longer a slave for my father, to be told what to do according to his whims. Some power had shifted from my father to me.

From that day on, if he wanted me to help with a chore, he asked. He no longer just told me what to do. (If he did, I would reply, "Sorry, I'm busy.") He'd ask, "Do you have time to dig some potatoes after supper?" And I would decide if I was free to help.

"The Legend of the Rake" was a key event in the development of my relationship with the world, and especially my relationship with my father. I don't think before this Dad even saw me as separate from him. I was just an extension of his being, under his total command, and he was in control of everything.

Dad does not remember thrashing me with the rake handle, and that's okay.

I remember.

I remember it well, because that was the last time he ever beat me.

I have spent hours in therapy reviewing this scene, handling it until the corners are worn smooth, reframing it into something fetching I can display like a trophy on my wall of healing. The symbolism was potent and the physical abuse undeniable. I felt the need to revisit both these aspects. I had earned a bit of freedom, but also several bruises.

The goal is to reach the point of forgiving myself, and forgiving my father. These few minutes of my young teenage life are seared into my emotional template, yet to my father, the scene did not even register. I suspect it is something he never even remembered for long. He did not get his way, and that is not something he would have dwelled on. No wonder he claims it never happened.

I remember feeling triumphant. Even then, I knew this defiant encounter with my father was no ordinary moment. I had stood up for myself and survived. I was bruised, and shaky, but exultant.

It was probably the endorphins.

I've been chasing them ever since.

As I write these words, I slowly realize that Dad likely has his wires crossed. The rebellious son story is probably not about my brother.

Around the time of the business with the rake, my mother told me that my father found me rebellious and did not know what to do with me. My mother certainly would have defended me. Did she forbid punishing her high-spirited baby? Is Dad's story about "the son he was forced to give up on" really about me after all?

That narrative makes much more sense.

He gave up on me, yes—gave up trying to control me. Because the way he had been going about it just wasn't working anymore.

Realizing that this story was about me all along—not my brother—is one of those incredibly obvious things that you just can't see. Until you do. And then you wonder how you never saw it before.

———

A COUPLE OF YEARS AGO I went with Dad to see a specialist, and several times in the following days, Dad asked me what the doctor had said. If Dad goes to an appointment and is then asked what the doctor told him, Dad just says, "Not much. Everything is fine." Unless someone goes with him, we have no idea what is going on. Dad deliberately minimizes, conveniently forgets, or least culpably—is simply unable to remember. Now, my brother and I try to attend Dad's appointments with him.

I drive Dad up to see his naturopath, a lovely silver-haired woman. Recently I threw out hundreds of dollars' worth of tonics and supplements Lois had recommended for Dad over the years. He would take her list to the health food store, buy whatever she suggested, bring the products home, and tuck them away in the cupboard. They sat there, untouched. Most of these packages were unopened and several years expired. I throw them all out when Dad is not looking.

Everyone calls the naturopath by her first name. Lois helps Dad remove his boots so she can check the swelling in his feet. "Your boots are so heavy, Stephen!"

"And they leak," Dad says. This is news to me.

While she takes his blood pressure, Lois asks my father how he has been, and he says, "Fine."

"Anything new?" she asks, and he says, "No."

This is why someone needs to go to medical appointments with my father. "Actually," I say, "he had what seems to have been a bladder infection, and is just finishing up some antibiotics."

Lois wants to know more. "A bladder infection, Stephen? That's unusual for you. What is going on?"

He looks at me. "You seem to know all about it," he says, and not in a nice way. There is an edge of disdain, or bitterness. I can tell he feels cornered.

"Dad has started wearing a product like Depends. He didn't really tell anyone he was doing this, so we weren't paying attention. He thinks they cost too much, so he wears the same one for more than one day."

"Oh, that's not good, Stephen. You should change them every day."

"Sometimes they're not dirty," Dad says. "They are still perfectly good."

"Doesn't matter," Lois says. "If you reuse them, you get things like bladder infections. Now I understand."

The ongoing saga of adult incontinence products is something I stumble into quite by accident (that is, if being nosy is an accident and not a lifestyle). Cathy casually mentioned taking Dad to the drugstore so he could buy his Depends and wondered, as if it was an afterthought, if they might have anything to do with his bladder infection.

We call this product Depends, which is a brand name, even though my father buys the cheaper drugstore brand.

When I hear he is using these products, immediately I am concerned. I ask, "What is he doing with the old ones?"

Cathy helps Dad buy them but apparently never wonders where they end up. Dad is a notorious hoarder—I find it hard to imagine he's just throwing these things away. An investigation reveals a stash of dirty Depends in a bag under his bed. Dad agrees to a new system of disposal, but through relentless monitoring, I soon discover that after Dad got dressed there is no used adult incontinence product in the garbage bag hanging from his bedroom door. Nor is anything stashed under his bed. Where did it go?

He admits to wearing the same one from yesterday. He prefers to reuse them, at least once.

It's unclear what prompted my father's decision to start wearing an adult incontinence product. Did he have an accident one day, unable to scuttle to the bathroom in time? My father smuggled these products into the house like contraband, hidden in a large shopping bag; took them right up to his room and stuffed them under his bed. He probably resents that my meddling has exposed his secret. But really, it was his bladder infection that made everyone start to ask questions.

His sons also have a secret—out of earshot we refer to the things he wears as diapers. Adult diapers.

You can see them under his jeans, his seat and hips puffy, like a toddler's.

Following his appointment with the naturopath, Dad schedules his next visit at reception. Another patient is also at the counter. She seems to be in a hurry.

Dad turns to this woman. "Do you garden?"

"No," she says, quite curtly, barely glancing at him before directing her attention back to the receptionist. Even in this small town, it is a clear breach of the rules of social distance to try to chat with a stranger at the counter of a medical clinic while they are involved in their own business.

Dad pays no attention to her body language. "I can show you my peanuts," he says. "Do you know where I live?"

"Sorry," the woman says. "I have to get back to work."

She really seems to be in a rush, but Dad barrels ahead with detailed directions.

"The first house past the intersection of Commercial and Main," Dad says. "On the left. Do you know where the store is? It's the driveway the other side of the store."

This woman is not playing along. She does not like being talked over and interrupted.

"I'm really not interested," she declares, her tone so stern and frosty that even Dad realizes the conversation is over.

Back in the van, driving home, I talk to Dad about what just happened.

"You're obsessed with peanuts," I say.

"I dare say that's true," Dad admits.

"You talk to people about peanuts whether they're interested or not."

"If they're not interested," he says, "they can always say no."

"That woman just now," I say. "She wasn't interested. She was saying no. And you just kept going. You were not listening to what she was saying."

"Uh-huh," Dad says, giving his two-syllable grunting sigh that indicates I am getting on his nerves.

I try to make my tone conversational, not accusatory. "I'm curious, Dad. Why did you keep persisting, even though she was busy and saying no?"

He pauses just long enough before answering. "That's a good question," he says.

And that's the strongest admission I will ever get from Dad that even he thinks his obsession with peanuts might sometimes go a little too far. If indeed that was an admission, and not merely an observation.

Here's what I see. Dad is lonely and has a shrinking social life, but all he wants to talk about if he meets people is peanuts. Are his encounters one-sided because he can't hear very well? Whatever the reason, he doesn't show much interest in other people. He won't listen to their stories. He just wants to talk about peanuts and sweet potatoes. Either he drives people away, or is indulged by those willing to shelter him in their kindness, and listen to his same old stories, walk with him to the garden to see his peanut plants or go on a tour of his almost empty greenhouse, at least fifteen or twenty times.

It makes him happy, they tell me, so why not?

He talks to strangers about peanuts and invites women over to the Wednesday night polka party but cannot on his own come up with other ways to address being lonely. I suggest he try attending the adult day program at the health centre, but Dad is insulted.

"That's for cripples," he says, appalled.

He looks shocked that I would even suggest such a thing. That I could imagine the program was suitable for him. I feel him shrinking away from me, as if I were dangerously delusional, maybe even contagious.

———

TODAY'S MISSION IS TO GET DAD NEW WINTER BOOTS. He claims he doesn't need new boots, even though the treads on his current pair are worn, and as he just mentioned they leak. His biggest fear is cold feet and his winter boots leak—you'd think he'd be anxious to get new ones. But no. He resists. He frets about the cost.

"Don't worry," I say. "I'll buy them as an early birthday present."

"Oh, Stephen, how lucky you are," Kim says. "You're so spoiled!"

Kim and I have planned this shopping trip to coincide with her work schedule. Having learned my lesson, I'll only take Dad shopping with his care worker—I need someone who can manage him. We're also going for jeans, at least two pairs, because one is almost always in the laundry. The girls do laundry constantly.

Dad is at the garage door when I come along with his walker.

"What's that for?" he says.

"We're taking it with us," I say. "Who knows how far we will have to walk in the mall to get to the shoe store."

"I don't need it," Dad says.

"You might, Stephen," Kim says. "You might get tired and need to sit down."

"I don't want it," Dad says. He sounds panicky.

We just look at him.

He moves over and plops down on the stool next to the door. "I'm not going." He points to the walker. "If you take that, I'm not going."

"Look Dad, you already agreed to go. This is the only day that fits in Kim's schedule before I'm gone. It has to be today."

Dad says he'll go if we leave the walker at home.

"This is for your safety, Dad. The doctor says you should use it. The OT said last year that you should be using a walker. We're going to a big mall, and there may be a lot of walking."

He's not budging.

My wall hits Dad's wall. My wall has words instead of bricks. That's the big difference between us—my wall talks.

"Okay, Dad. This is the way it is. This is not me saying to do something. This is advice coming from medical professionals who are concerned with your safety. If you are not willing to follow reasonable advice from people who are trying to help you, you may not be able to keep living in this house. The real issue we are facing is this—can you make good decisions? If you demonstrate you can make good decisions, great. But if you cannot show you are capable of making good decisions, then I'm sorry—but maybe you're no longer capable of living here in this house."

Dad has gotten to his feet during my tirade, provoked by my hectoring tone. He is standing now, facing me. He is so furious his eyes are afire but he cannot find any words. He raises his cane and holds it up horizontally in front of him. Both fists, white-knuckled, quiver.

This is a tense moment. But Dad has prepared me for such an encounter. I do not flinch or back down. I'm amazed how calm I am.

"You touch me with that cane and you'll wish you hadn't," I say.

He shakes with frustration, but I see him wilting.

"Now, Stephen." Kim steps in to soothe him. "Why are you upset? We're just going to the mall and do a little shopping. It'll be fun. C'mon, get your coat on. Is this the jacket you want to wear? It's colder than it looks. The wind is cold. Here, let me help you with that jacket."

We load Dad into the passenger seat of the van and the sturdy sleek walker folds up and stands just inside the sliding door, next to Kim in the back seat.

Later, Kim says to me, "It really looked like your father was going to clobber you with his cane."

Dad tells me how to get to Greenwood, as if I have never driven there before. I prefer the old number one highway, which I used to travel every day in high school. I wonder if Dad likes his particular route to avoid driving past the spot where my mother had her accident. In my fantasy world, he tells me things like: "Don't take the number one. It reminds me how Chris died." Just simple things that allow me to glimpse the inner workings of his soul.

Instead, he issues directions and expects to be obeyed. He thinks being old is an ordeal ("Do you want some advice?" he loves to ask. "Never grow old."), but in many ways—that he fails to notice or appreciate—the whole world revolves around him. Just a simple trip to buy boots and jeans has involved days of planning and a big fight. Nothing is simple with Dad.

At the Greenwood Mall I unload the walker and Dad uses it. His mood now has flipped to stoic and aggrieved. Kim walks with him, resting her hand on top of his. One reason he does not want to use a walker, according to Kim, is that he enjoys holding hands with the girls and doesn't want to give that up. She makes a point of walking with him, touching and distracting him as necessary.

At the shoe store we find a nice pair of winter boots. These North Face hiking boots are designed for the cold and extremely light. When Dad tries them out, using his walker, Kim and I are astonished to actually see the soles of his boots.

"Look at that," Kim marvels. "He's picking up his feet!"

These expensive boots are fifty percent off. The stars have aligned.

Dad is embarrassed to be seen with the walker but he endures. We stop at the food court for a drink, something Kim had told Dad she wanted to do (a subplot in today's episode of "Let's Try to Take Dad Shopping").

Dad sees someone he seems to know. It is always the same when Dad runs into someone. They will talk for a bit and say goodbye, and then Dad will turn to me and ask, "Who was that?" Of course I have no idea.

On the way back to the van, Dad uses the brakes on the walker to go down a ramp that otherwise he would have needed assistance with.

"Your father's a pro with the walker," Kim whispers.

We have walked a fair distance, and he does not seem tired.

We drive over to Mark's for the jeans. Kim and I start sifting through the stacks, and then she nudges me and nods towards my father. He is sitting in his walker. So much fuss about how he did not need it, but one minute into shopping for jeans and he is using it to take a break. It provides a good seat for him, fairly high, and now the handles are armrests he can use to help push himself back up. His upper body strength has always been good, but his legs have gotten weak. He needs to be prompted, though, to lock the brakes before using the walker as a seat.

Sitting there, he looks serene and a little detached, a little self-conscious, like a cat in the litter box.

Kim takes Dad and his walker into the change room to try on some jeans and we manage to find a couple of pairs everyone deems acceptable. There is no talk of an eleven-inch zipper this time around. That's the thing with Dad—he goes through these obsessions, and then they pass.

Except for peanuts, of course.

Peanuts are forever.

My father keeps complaining about my brother being stubborn.

I have to laugh. "Who does he get that from?" I ask. "Who do you think he takes after?"

I can see he's on the verge of blaming our dead mother, so I say it first. "Look at Mom. She was stubborn as hell. But what do you think you're like? You're even more stubborn. We're all stubborn. Where do you think I got it from? Before you start complaining about your sons, ask yourself: Who do we take after? You know what they say—the apple doesn't fall far from the tree."

I am stubborn. I am determined. If I decide something is for Dad's own good, I will do that thing even if he doesn't want it to happen. I decide that I know better. This is what parenting is about, and this is also eldercare. The roles have flipped, except I cannot ground Dad, or take the TV away, or send him to his room.

I probably shouldn't even whack him with a broomstick.

I can only threaten him with juvie—I mean, a home. Not his home, but a home.

It's amazing, isn't it? The difference between *home*, and *a home*.

Dad was always a sort of tyrant and now he is a frustrated tyrant. He does not accept the view that we are all in orbit around him. From his perspective, he is the victim. People do not obey his commands.

They ignore his wishes. They bully him into doing things he does not want to do. They hide his boots—his favourite old heavy work-boots that he would slip into without tying the laces and scuff along.

And when I say "they" hid his boots, I mean me. I hid his boots.

I have learned that a person can reach a point in life where it seems necessary to hide his father's favourite old boots.

Out the window this morning I watch my father shuffle to the greenhouse in his old boots. I remember how excited Kim and I were at the store to see Dad's soles when he walked. When he used to walk all the time, it was fine to slip on untied boots and drag his feet over to the greenhouse. But now that is all he does. Most days, that's as far as he goes. His mobility is rapidly getting carved into a groove. Into a small sad rut of his own creation. He is on the verge of losing the ability to do anything but shuffle. Dad resists using the walker, but does not realize how close he is to not even being able to use a walker.

And so I hide his old boots, just before I leave for Vancouver. I tell Kim and my brother what I have done and say, "Blame it on me."

Kim says, "Don't tell me where you hid them. I don't want to lie."

It's cruel, manipulative, and deceitful—yes, all of those things.

All is fair in love and war, and this is both.

This is the war of the walker, and this is my one last manoeuvre, for now, as I prepare to leave the field of battle.

———

BACK IN VANCOUVER, in the noise of the outside world, my sensible boss offers his perspective on the confusing priorities of eldercare.

"Look at it this way," he says, "if your father falls on his way to the greenhouse, at least he'll have died with his boots on."

Those half-price North Face hiking boots are not subjected to the most demanding conditions. They are worn by a man in his nineties who uses a walker, plodding and scuffing short distances during nicer weather, on sidewalks that have been cleared of snow. And yet in only a few months his new boots start to fall apart.

Nothing is built to last anymore, and this is what bothers Dad the most. He liked his new boots, once he got used to them. But boots should last. Boots should last a lifetime. At his age, he sure never expected to outlive his brand new boots.

The disappearance of Dad's favourite old boots is blamed on George.

I hear reports that Dad keeps threatening to call and find out what I did with his boots, but guess what?

He never does.

5

WHAT NEXT

Confabulate: In psychology, to compensate for loss or impairment of memory by fabrication or invention of details.

WHEN I RETURN TO NOVA SCOTIA, six months later, Dad fills me in on how great it is to use the walker. He explains he is walking more, and that has made him stronger. He tells me getting the walker is the best decision he ever made. He makes it sound like it was his idea all along, and I am the stubborn holdout who still needs convincing.

For once I bite my savage tongue. He's using the walker—that's what's important. And it helps him be social. If he goes for an outing and runs into someone, he can sit and rest while they talk.

The walker has changed his life. Surely, that is more important than me getting any sort of recognition. Right? Seriously, I do not want the credit for pushing Dad into doing something that actually turned out to be good for him.

The goal was for him to use the walker. Knowing Dad is walking more is reward enough. Really, I don't need the credit for being right all along. I don't need him to utter the briefest syllable of thanks, or make the slightest acknowledgment that maybe, sometimes, I know enough about the world to help him a tiny bit. No, I would not want any of that.

Gratitude would be too much of a shock to my system.

———

ONE OF THE YOUNGER, MORE WORLDLY GIRLS says she is worried about my father. He shows no discernment when talking to people about peanuts. He will invite simply anyone home to see his peanuts. His open-minded attitude may be saintly, but the girls are concerned for his safety and also their own. Only one care worker is here at a time, alone with Dad in the house, and the door is never locked during the day. When he drags strangers home, everyone is exposed to a degree of risk. He brings all sorts of people right into the house, and he does not discriminate. This is beautiful, right? Let me give you an example.

Today, on Dad's walk with his care worker, they came across a young woman wearing pyjamas in the parking lot of the store who was cleaning fast-food garbage out of her car. She might have been living in her car, it was so crammed with stuff—and remember, she was in her pyjamas. Frantically sorting and throwing out trash, all the while picking at bloody sores on her face.

Dad spots this young woman, revs up the walker, and beelines over to her. Busy teasing fresh blood out of a scab on her face, she barely listens to my father as he invites her home to see his peanuts.

Dad's lack of judgment made the care worker uncomfortable. That young woman, digging through the junk in her car, "looked very sketchy." The care worker wants me to talk to my father.

I am flattered by her faith in my influence with Dad.

I decide to approach the situation as a safety issue for the girls—not as a criticism of his peanut obsession. Going up against the peanuts would be a losing battle, but Dad is naturally inclined to be protective of his care team. I'll have to work along with Dad's emotional gravity if things are going to fall my way.

"Do you remember talking to a woman over at the store today?" I ask.

"What woman?"

"In the parking lot. You wanted to show her your peanuts."

"Oh, yes," Dad says. "She was too busy."

"Did you notice her picking at the sores on her face?"

Dad says yes.

"Do you know what that might mean?"

Dad shakes his head.

"Well, Dad, often it means that the person is involved with drugs. Scabs like that could mean the person is on drugs."

"I noticed the scabs," Dad says, "but I had no idea."

"Did you notice she was wearing pyjamas outside in the middle of the day?"

"Yes," Dad says, "but that doesn't matter. I thought she might want to see my peanuts."

"Someone like that might think you live alone, and then come back later with her drug addict boyfriend."

"I never thought of that," Dad says.

"You need to be careful who you invite home," I say. "You need to think of the girls. We can't have the wrong kind of people looking around and getting ideas."

"Okay," Dad says. "I'll have to be more careful."

Well that went surprisingly well. Although I doubt our little talk will change anything. Dad is powerless over peanuts.

During the summer Dad mostly just invites people to the small garden next to the driveway to admire his peanut plants. But year round he keeps entire dried plants in the garage so he can wave them around in front of astonished crowds.

Hopefully, Dad's world view will insulate him. He does not live in the cynical world of fear and paranoia. Bless his heart; except for that lapse around the disappearance of his beloved popcorn, Dad does not normally dwell in a fearful suspicious world.

So far, Dad has avoided trouble. Perhaps his innocence meets its match. Perhaps only the right sort of person agrees to be shown an old man's peanuts.

Nothing bad has happened and we are trying to keep it that way.

His innocence, I fear, is his most fragile possession.

Another of Dad's habits shows his trusting nature.

If you stop at my brother's store, you may be surprised when you return to your vehicle to find my father sitting in your passenger seat waiting for his driver.

This is most likely to happen if you are driving a van. Dad will climb into a van, possibly because he thinks it is my brother's.

When the stranger returns and utters a surprised and questioning "Hello?"—Dad will say, "I want to go up town."

There is a certain freedom in being old. You are cut a lot of slack. You can climb into a stranger's van and he will give you a ride up town. After dropping you off, he'll drive back to the store to tell my brother, "I just drove your father up to the grocery store. At least I think it was your father. I hope that's okay."

"He'll be fine," my brother will say. "With the way my luck's been going—someone will bring him back."

Freedom cuts through all restraints but is a double-edged sword. You have the freedom to say whatever you want, but people may not take you seriously. They may only pretend to listen. If you're old, you have the freedom to be humoured.

Not being taken seriously can be a good thing if you are incredibly rude. Dad is rudest to his family (my brother and me) and polite to strangers. "This is perfectly normal," I am told again and again by everyone who works with generations of adults. "Don't take it personally," I am told. *Don't take it personally when your very own father is a crusty old son of a bitch.*

The tendency is to be meanest to those who are closest. It is a display of great love, cruel love, tough love—love in one of its harshest manifestations. It is a love that makes it easier to contemplate life after they are gone.

———

THE FRONT DOORBELL RINGS early one evening. My brother goes to see who it is. Someone is looking for a Main Street address on Commercial Street. Happens all the time. My brother is pointing them in the right direction when my father totters up and interrupts.

"What are you looking for?" Dad asks.

"Don't worry about it," my brother says. "It's all taken care of."

"You be quiet," Dad says.

"Go sit down," my brother says right back, his tone of voice matching our father's. My brother then turns back around to talk to the abashed strangers who rang the wrong doorbell.

Dad makes a noise like he's trying to speak but nothing can come out. He hauls off and whacks my brother's upper back as hard as he can. Hitting my brother is like hitting a wall. My brother does not move, but the rebound of his own blow almost knocks my father over. He staggers backwards. Luckily, Kim had followed him to the door and is able to steady him.

My brother is angry now, too. "You hit me again," he tells Dad, "and you'll be in a home so fast your head will spin."

Kim leads Dad to his chair, and my brother finishes giving directions.

This ugly little scene speaks to decades of frustration and anger. Dad's impulse to control everything is relentless. I cannot step out of the kitchen with an empty jar without facing an interrogation. My brother cannot point the way in the town where he has lived his entire life without Dad trying to butt in and take over.

And before you know it, Dad would have been talking to the strangers at the door about peanuts. That's probably what this whole little episode was really about: Dad sensing an opportunity to show off his peanut plants, and my brother dreading the unrelenting, mortifying shame.

My brother and I worry about the direction Dad is headed. When we were kids Dad was quick to slap us or grab our arms in his painful grip. The aging process, in a way, is a progression back in time. Is our father going to revert to walloping us if he feels frustrated or disrespected? Is it only my brother and I who are at risk, or might Dad strike a care worker too when his temper flares?

One quiet afternoon I attempt to talk to Dad.

"It must be frustrating," I say, "to not be able to do everything you used to."

He looks at me, his gaze unreadable.

"Even at my age, I notice it," I say. "I'm not as young as I used to be. I can't play tennis like I used to."

"You might be surprised what I can still do." Dad does his best to make this sound like a threat.

"Part of aging though, is accepting the changes. Don't you think, Dad?"

"I guess so," he says.

"There's no point fighting against the things you can't control."

"I have to fight," Dad says. "No one else will."

"But maybe you are fighting for something that is already gone."

"What do you mean?"

"Like all that stuff in the garage you were upset about. What does that stuff mean to you?"

Dad draws a blank on this. My question lacks a concrete image. There's no point being vague and open-ended.

I try again. "Don't you think that part of the reason you were upset is because you were dealing with the idea that you are no longer going to work as an electrician? That you have to let that part of your life go?"

There is a moment of silence as the words percolate.

Then he says, "Maybe," but I cannot tell how much of what I said he is prepared to take seriously.

I've had some therapy, and think nothing of going to an inner child workshop, an emotional process weekend, or a gong bath. (Yes, in my outside world we have such a thing as a gong bath. One bathes one's aura in the reverberations of a resounding gong. The experience can be akin to shamanic journeying, accompanied by the gong instead of a drum.)

If I'm not careful to avoid jargon and shorthand, I risk speaking a nonsensical "healing journey" language foreign to my father's ears.

Who knows what my father hears when I talk, but I persist in discussing what he is going through, what we all must go through. Otherwise there is little chance any of us will ever find a light in the darkness.

———

THERE IS A NEW CREW OF GIRLS NOW. Kim left the company she worked for, and her rapport with Dad was the only reason we had put off switching to a new agency. The old company had staffing and management problems, and sent over inexperienced workers. If a new worker showed up, one who had never even met my father before, it was up to Dad to provide the orientation. You can imagine how well that went. First, she gets the full peanut experience, which consumes about half the shift, and then Dad will insist on a complete fabrication like, "Today is not bath day. I just had one yesterday."

If Dad is meeting a care worker for the first time, he prefers to sit and talk a bit before getting completely naked. He's old-fashioned that way.

Don't get me wrong—showing up at a stranger's house and being expected to clean, do laundry, maybe help with bathing and dressing, and make a meal, all in two hours, is definitely a challenge. Above all, the care worker must manage the client, who often has cognitive impairments, and that requires tact, flexibility, and social acuity. The skill set demanded of these care workers is enormous.

The new care agency is partly worker owned, and a higher level of professionalism is immediately apparent. If a new worker joins Dad's care team, there is a training shift with a worker who already knows

Dad's routine. A registered nurse is available by phone twenty-four hours a day. A large binder on top of the fridge details every aspect of Dad's care.

The new main care worker is Angela, who arrives like a large, warm, beating heart, pumping life right into the family. She transforms the house and takes the best care of Dad. We all fall in love with her a bit. She's there to care for Dad but firmly believes that taking care of his family is also helping Dad. She cooks for everyone. She even insists on doing my laundry and cheerfully blows past my token protests.

Some of the previous care workers did not share this attitude. One of the least helpful tried to pick through seven dirty breakfast dishes in order to only wash the ones Dad used personally. It took more time trying to separate the dishes than it would have to just wash them all. Dad stood next to her by the sink and kept handing her my brother's cereal bowl. She'd put it down and he'd pick it up and hand it to her again, expecting her to wash it. She didn't last long. Even Dad thought she was next to useless.

Angela is a breath of fresh air and her lively spirit touches us all. But she has her quirks too, which add to her charm.

"Some of the other girls don't do it the right way," Angela says, refolding towels to show how it should be done. "But I am very particular."

With a small, regular crew there is more time to get to know one another. I spend of lot of time with the caregivers, because I visit for around three weeks at a time, and they are in the house every day. We often cook together, and I hear stories about my father while he naps.

He's become remarkably candid about his personal life. Dad confided to Angela that his wife was going to leave him before she died.

"That's right," I say. "She was going to leave. For twenty years, she was going to leave."

About my sister, my eldest sibling, born out of wedlock, Dad says, "The wife got a head start with Sandra. Had her before we got married."

Chatting with Angela about what Dad has been telling her forces me to think about my family—what to tell and what to hold back. It is a challenge to shape our messy history into a pleasing package.

The following chunk covers a good deal of ground, summarizing hours of kitchen conversation with caregivers. I'm thinking of calling it "Frozen Smiles"—but ignore that. I'm mad for titles, but nothing is more boring than a writer writing about writing. Just read it, and you might understand a bit more. You'll never understand everything, but you will understand more.

———

MY FATHER'S PARENTS DISAPPROVED so strongly of my mother (viewed, without doubt, as a social inferior and even worse, as a slut) that running off together was the only option. My mother managed to spin this tale into a romantic kind of thing—eloping and honeymooning at the tiny cottage perched close to the wharf in Harbourville, on the tide-worn coast of the Bay of Fundy. It seems funny to honeymoon only ten minutes away, but that is what they did. Eloped, and honeymooned in Harbourville, of all places.

My father was in the volunteer fire department. Not sure who witnessed their bare-bones wedding, but fire department members got involved and at the weathered grey honeymoon cottage they short-sheeted the bed.

Long after my mother died and turned into a saintly wife and the love of his life, my father told me they got married "to give Sandy a home." Sandra was my mother's child, an unwelcome little burden being raised by my mother's parents. (Or, rather, by my mother's mother, and her second—or third—husband, depending how you conduct the count.)

My father said he wanted to give Sandra a home because "things weren't good on the farm with her grandmother." When Sandra was very young she was left alone with the washing machine, an old wringer washer—"Your grandmother was out in the barn with a man"—and Sandra's arm got caught, and wrung. Massive scarring, operations, skin grafts, the works. Her upper arm looked like it had been made from a thick fibrous angry liquid, churned up and reset-tled into a rough streaky solid.

My father tells me this story—"Why I married your mother"—more than twenty-five years after my sister Sandra killed herself. He has not mentioned her name for many years, but her frozen smiles are framed and line the red-brick mantel. His care workers have been asking about the young woman in the photos. They tell me he says his daughter, Sandra, who was officially adopted after the wedding, died of cancer.

I raise my eyebrows at Angela. "Cancer? Is that what he says?"

Then we just look at each other. I don't say anything, but some-how I feel she understands.

"Not cancer," she says quietly.

"Nope." I furiously peel a carrot.

I wonder if Dad honestly believes my sister died of cancer, or if that is only what he says to cover up a more uncomfortable truth.

Maybe he has been telling the cancer story for so many years, he finally believes it himself.

I'm not going to ask.

We all have things we need to believe.

———

DAD IS NOT WEARING HIS HEARING AIDS, so my brother and I only have to lower our voices to speak in complete privacy right in front of him.

Talking around Dad is easy, but actually trying to communicate with him is another matter. A few days into my visit I become frustrated.

"WHY DON'T YOU WEAR YOUR HEARING AIDS?" I yell. "I'M TIRED OF YELLING."

"You don't have to yell," Dad says.

"So I should just speak normally?" I ask Dad, speaking normally. "Huh?"

"This is speaking normally," I say.

"What?" He cups his ear.

I spend some time shouting at him, trying to convince him to wear his hearing aids.

He says, "They don't work."

"DO THEY NEED CLEANING?"

"No."

"DO YOU CLEAN THEM?"

"They don't have to be cleaned," Dad tells me.

I'm naturally suspicious of this claim, since Dad can be unreliable.

Plus, when going through stacks of mail, I noticed the hearing aid store had sent Dad a birthday card—with a coupon for a free cleaning.

Dad bought these hearing aids all on his own, without shopping around or talking to anyone. He took the bus to Kentville, lured by a sale price of $1,500, and was talked into spending $6,000. He claims the salesperson told him Veterans Affairs would pay for them. The store gave him a number to call, but it had nothing to do with Veterans Affairs. I tried calling it myself and it was a residence. I don't know what these scammers actually told Dad, but he certainly believed Veterans Affairs would refund all the money. They either lied to him or took advantage of his confusion. Probably both.

I find the free cleaning coupon and we drive into Kentville. The hearing aid store is in the Cornwallis Inn, an ornate old Tudoresque concrete and brick edifice that attempts to dignify Kentville. Dad instructs me which lane to be in to make the left turn into the parking lot. This left turn suddenly feels very familiar. My many trips to the ground-floor liquor store carved the route into my teenage brain. The Kentville liquor store, notoriously lax on asking for ID, was the booze hookup for many avid underage drinkers. My borrowed ID, slipped from my brother's wallet without his knowledge, gave me enough confidence that the package store, as the old-timers called it, rarely asked me for proof of age. Certainly they didn't in Kentville.

My father and I take an elevator up to a suite of offices. The villain in the hearing aid story immediately becomes apparent—the sales rep who smiles at Dad and touches him on the shoulder. She is the one responsible for convincing a vulnerable old man to part with thousands of dollars for a fancy device he really didn't need. Of course, it is Dad's fault too, for not doing any market research, for not taking a shopping buddy, for being penny-wise and pound foolish. Is he to blame as well for being lonely and susceptible to a stranger's charms? I despise this smarmy outgoing sales rep, with her fake nails and fake hair, even though she thinks I am Dad's grandson. This is perhaps a tiny misstep, because Dad's vanity is stung.

The sales rep flatters me at the risk of offending Dad. He's already under her spell and now she wants to win me over. Good luck, lady—you're barking up the wrong tree. I cannot forgive her for taking advantage of a lonely ninety-year-old, and smiling all the way through her well-oiled sales pitch.

The hearing aids do indeed need cleaning. They are clogged with an old man's exuberant earwax, and have a little doodad that needs regular replacement. The sales rep goes over everything she told Dad before, none of which he remembered.

"Do you use the remote control, Stephen?" she asks.

"Shush, don't tell him," Dad says, tilting his head towards where I am sitting in the waiting area.

I pretend not to be listening but am fit to be tied. This is the first I have heard of a remote control. I had asked Dad if his hearing aids were adjustable and he said no, they were simply turned on by inserting the battery. Now I learn Dad is supposed to clean his hearing aids every day, and they have features he has no idea how to use. Fake-hair-and-nails told him all this before and, what's more, expected he would hear and remember.

When we get back to the house I march right up to Dad's bedroom and rummage through the shopping bag that came with all the hearing aid gear. Everything is still in the bag, naturally, because in this house nothing is discarded. There is a remote control, still in the box, completely untouched. There is an instruction manual, which Dad has not bothered to look at. The volume for the hearing aids can be adjusted. There are different operating modes depending on the type and level of background noise. In fact, there are so many features the hearing aids are actually too complicated for Dad to operate. One would need to carry around the hefty instruction manual just to figure out the tiny remote control.

Dad peruses sales flyers every week so he might save three dollars at the grocery store, yet spends $6,000 for hearing aids as an impulse purchase and then never bothers to learn how the damn things work or how to take care of them. He said they weren't working and just gave up on them. The instruction manual, had it been given a glance, would have pointed to the problem.

Hearing aid maintenance gets added to the list of chores for other people to take care of.

I refuse to spend another penny at the place that ripped off my father, so I buy a stock of batteries at the drugstore. Now Dad has no excuse. The batteries are a small price to pay to be able to talk in a normal voice. If Dad can't hear me, I yell, "DO YOU HAVE YOUR HEARING AIDS IN?"

He starts to wear them more regularly—with a little prompting. We experiment with the remote control, but he never learns how to use it.

Now that talking is easier, I'm having richer conversations with Dad, especially about the old days. Dad claims to have a memory from when he was eighteen months old. He was sitting under a quilting frame, tugging at loose threads. He can remember everything from eighty or ninety years ago. It is only yesterday that escapes him.

Dad tells me how they used to cut hay down by the river with a team of horses. The ground was marshy, so they had to strap wooden horseshoes on the team. He says the wooden horseshoes looked like snowshoes, but smaller. Same idea, though—they kept the horses from sinking into the soft surface.

"That's something you don't see anymore," Dad says, somewhat wistfully.

I'm already busy at my laptop, because I'm a curious George. I find an online archive of a newspaper in Indiana with a story from the 1930s about horse teams with wooden horseshoes. Along with the text, there are pictures of the team of horses at work and a close-up of a wooden horseshoe. Leather straps secure the shoe, which is about twice as wide as the hoof.

"Does this look right?" I take my laptop over to Dad's chair.

He is speechless. He looks from the computer to me and back to the screen. He seems awestruck. "You have all that in there?"

I explain the computer did a search, and we are looking at a newspaper archive stored somewhere in the world, who knows where.

"What next," he says, incredulous.

I make the pictures larger, so he can better see the grainy close-up of the wooden horseshoe.

"That's it," he says softly.

I notice he is tearing up. He wipes his face.

"What's going on, Dad?" I ask gently, afraid to squash the moment but too inquisitive to leave it alone.

"Never thought I would see something like that again," he says. "Boy oh boy, that's something. That's really something."

Over the next several days, he often revisits this wondrous moment. "I sure never expected to see wooden horseshoes again," he says. His delicate heartfelt words make the sight of wooden horseshoes on a working team seem like a tiny miracle.

Maybe, to him, it was.

MY FATHER HAS A SURPRISING QUESTION FOR ME.

"If I got remarried," he says, "would you approve?"

"That depends," I say.

"On what?"

"If she was good for you."

He seems satisfied.

"Do you have anyone in mind?" I ask.

"No," he says. "Just wondering what you thought."

The topic surprises me because it has never been broached before. My mother died twenty-five years ago.

"You were only sixty-nine when Mom died," I say. "How come you never talked about getting remarried before?"

"Never found the right person," Dad explains. I'm a little amazed by his ready answer. But wait, there's more: "Or else she wasn't interested. Or she was already married."

Dad has a list of prospects? Has he tried to court a woman, and been rejected? Was he chasing married women? Dad used to be cool and distant around women, seemingly oblivious to any overtures. In his seventies, for example, as a fairly recent widower, he simply did not seem interested. Lately, though, he has become more flirtatious. Being touched by the girls has awakened something in him. He has remembered some experience of tenderness he did not even realize he was missing.

Later, one of brother's friends tells me what my father said to her one day. "Your father asked me, he said, 'If I got remarried do you think I could find a woman who cooks without salt?'"

I ALWAYS DO THE COOKING when I come home, and I still help the caregivers. We cook together, or else I will cook and the caregiver is freed up to go for a walk with Dad, perhaps to visit the greenhouse, or just socialize with him.

Doing the cooking is a role I assigned myself. When I was about thirteen, my sister left home and my mother was working as a care aide at Grand View Manor, a home for seniors. With no women in the house to feed them, the men were suddenly helpless. I judged my father's and my brother's pathetic helplessness. I was not the type of person who needed a woman to feed me. I did not accept gender roles. To me, gender roles are a self-imposed, imaginary prison. I was much more practical than that. I wanted to eat, so naturally I started to cook.

Almost immediately Dad was looking to me for food.

My father loves his meals, so cooking gives me power. I can impose rules and standards of cleanliness in the kitchen and around food. Because I make the meals, I can be the boss in the kitchen.

So, yeah, I can cook. I've cooked in restaurants. I was a wok cook in a Thai/Caribbean restaurant, so I can make lemon coriander chicken, Thai peanut sauce, jerk chicken, or pad Thai for twenty.

When I first discovered Thai peanut sauce, it felt like the grown-up version of a kid's favourite food—peanut butter, with spices! I thought peanut sauce would be a special treat for Dad, but he found it too spicy even though I totally toned it down. He does not like that much flavour.

If you keep it simple, Dad eats whatever you put in front of him. When he's done he'll look at me.

"What next, George?"

"What do you want?"

"What have you got?"

"Well, there's yogurt," I say. "You could have yogurt and bananas."

"Sounds good," Dad says.

———

ONE DAY I ASK MY BROTHER, "When did Dad become so fond of kids?"

When we were young there was no indication Dad liked children. He was never one for holding and cuddling. Never seemed like he wanted to be around babies. But as soon as he turned ninety, look out. He's all about the kids.

As long as they aren't his own.

This softer, more emotional aspect to my father is fascinating but also puzzling. Is it hormonal? A symptom of decline? No longer able to control much of his life, he has become more reflective and sentimental.

When I visited in the fall of 2010, Dad was ninety-one and depressed. "This is not living," he said to me. He was lonely, socially isolated, and totally lacking the skills and insight to address the situation in any meaningful way.

I refer to this as my "first trip," but of course it was not. I had been visiting fairly regularly, making a trip to Nova Scotia every four or five years. The trip in 2010 was the first of many trips over the next few years, mostly every six months. My preference was to visit Dad in the spring and fall. I was avoiding winter, avoiding mosquitos, and avoiding visiting a sweltering and stuffy old house in summer where I was not allowed to open a window.

I started calling this fall 2010 visit my first trip, though, because it was my first eldercare trip.

My first trip was planned for one week. I stayed for three.

Dad was so rigid in his thinking, so securely in his rut, he could not even admit there was a problem. I was trying to get him to sign up for Meals on Wheels, but he kept saying, "Let's wait and see what happens."

"Wait and see what, exactly?" I said. "You have waited. You've already done that. This is what happens: you eating Pizza Pops and picking at a roast chicken from the deli counter and making it last a week."

It took two weeks, but Dad finally agreed to a trial delivery from Meals on Wheels. We split it up and shared it. It was actually quite good—basic, but real food, like a homecooked meal.

Dad was sold.

And just like that, his life improved a tiny bit. Now he had a schedule, someone dropping by three times a week, something to look forward to and plan his days around.

And he was eating better.

It was heartbreaking, actually, to see how much it meant for Dad to have someone stop by for no more than a minute or two. It was the highlight of his day, and a glimpse into how he was when I'm not here. He'd park himself in the chair by the front door and wait forty-five minutes for the volunteer to arrive with his meal.

Of course, if Dad was really lucky, he'd also get to talk about peanuts.

———

IN TERMS OF FOOD VALUE, Dad says peanuts are number two in the world.

He has some story about a medical problem—he was anemic, I think. They gave him steroids and he claims he was not properly warned that if you took the medication too long you could get cataracts.

Anyway, he starting taking peanut butter and was soon off the steroids.

But not soon enough. He had cataracts.

Whenever Dad says that peanuts are number two in terms of food value, I cannot resist. I always ask, "What is number one?"

He doesn't know. He stops to think about it but never can remember. He's not sure he ever really knew. But he knows for certain peanuts are number two. He's definite about that much. Number two in the world.

I didn't attend any appointments with Dad's eye doctor, so maybe I am the only one surprised by the amount of aftercare following cataract surgery.

The procedure is deemed perfectly safe, yet only one eye is done at a time, just in case. Immediately after each surgery, there is a regime of eye ointments and lubricating eye drops, applied almost continuously.

The ointment is the trickiest. The theory is simple—pull down the lower eyelid and use the little tube to squirt in a gob. But the thick ointment is too stubborn to squirt. It oozes out and hangs there like a greasy worm.

Angela makes it look easy. She keeps talking Dad through it, so he can do it himself before bed, and on the upcoming holiday. The budget doesn't cover care worker support on every holiday, which is another reason I come home for Easter and Thanksgiving.

Dad wants me to watch but is determined he can do it himself. He stands in front of the bathroom mirror, pulling down on the loose skin over his cheekbone. When the tip of the tube gets close, oozing ointment, Dad blinks. Every time. The ointment gets hung up in his eyelashes, and he smears it all around with his finger trying to mash the oily blob into his eye.

Then Dad totally surprises me. He asks for my help.

The job of applying the bedtime ointment falls to me, and on the holiday, I do it all day.

As with much of life, the key is confidence.

I learn not to hesitate, to squeeze with brisk enthusiasm. It is satisfying to deposit the oily worm in the pink pocket of Dad's lower eyelid, anointing his new eyesight.

I notice Dad lingering over the newspaper, rather than just flipping through it, and realize how much his vision has improved. Working on his puzzles must have been like peering through a keyhole. I have fresh appreciation for his focus and tenacity.

The ointment is only needed for a few weeks, and the lubricating eye drops taper off to twice a day. Twice a day, forever.

Drops in his eyes are added to the lengthening list of daily chores.

Dad lies on the chesterfield, a tissue ready in his hand.

Two drops in each eye.

Most of it goes in—unless he happens to blink. That is what the tissue is for.

What a sequence—steroids, then peanut butter, now eye drops.

There are so many of these complicated little developments and it is impossible to see them coming. Everything about aging and eldercare is totally predictable, yet the whole experience manages to completely surprise.

No wonder Dad keeps saying "What next" with such ennui, resignation, disbelief, and awe.

———

THE MORNING AFTER I ARRIVED on my first trip, Dad wanted to go grocery shopping. I said I had to clean first. I had to clean the fridge. "I'm not putting groceries in that fridge," I said.

Inside the fridge was covered with dead fruit flies.

Hundreds of them.

The house was infested. I made a trap and caught a bunch of larger ones, and the fruit flies kept getting smaller and smaller—but they also kept coming. Where were they coming from?

I investigated, searching for the fruit fly factory. In the basement, I found the problem. Dad had left some turnips (I think) in the cold room in plastic grocery bags. He had probably intended to deal with the produce later but then forgot. This was October—they were not from this year. The rank brown slime in the bags appeared to have already been processed through a digestive tract. That is a polite way to say it looked exactly like shit, and smelled even worse. Putrefaction slid from the bags and seeped into wooden crates. All this disgusting mess had to be hauled out of the cold room, up out of the basement, and taken outdoors.

The house immediately felt cleaner.

The fruit fly situation improved rapidly, but the cleanup in the cold room was just beginning. What else might be sitting in there, rotting? There were rows of bottled preserves, decades old, which should never be eaten. What about in the back corner, under that pile of boxes? Oh yes, the tub of beans.

I recognized this tub. It was the perforated tub from a large old automatic washing machine that Dad had repurposed to store dried beans. He grew long rows of Jacob's Cattle beans every year, and they were a lot of work. They had to be planted, and weeded, and then in the fall, once the plants had died and the bean shells were dry, the beans had to be harvested. All this work was done by hand. Sometimes the entire plants had to be pulled and dried indoors if the weather did not cooperate. Once the plants dried enough, indoors or out, we had discovered the easiest way to get the beans out of the shells was to hold the plants by the main stem and whack the top part of the plants against a big board. We used the headboard of the garden trailer, and the beans flew out of the dry shells and collected in the trailer bed.

More than little white-and-maroon beans collected in the trailer. Dirt and leaves and stems and weeds were all mixed with the beans.

The work, really, was just beginning.

The beans had to be cleaned. On a breezy day, you could try winnowing out the dirt or frig around using a screen of some sort, but mostly you ended up picking through and handling almost every single bean. Nothing less than perfection was acceptable to Dad—all the dirt had to be removed and not a single bean discarded in the process. Of course there are machines to do this job, but why spend money when your kids work for free? This was painstaking and incredibly boring. It was high on my list of most detested jobs—though I must admit, the top of that list was very crowded.

The whole process was heavily dependent on child labour, and even then there was no money in it. Dad sold some of these beans for pennies a pound. When I go to a grocery store today, decades later, and handle a pound of premium organic beans priced at $2.89, I think about how those two or three cups of dried beans would have taken so many tedious, back-breaking hours to plant, weed, harvest, clean, and sort.

The old washing machine tub in the cold room held a massive stash of vintage Jacob's Cattle. The beans are white and all shades of maroon, and the top layer looked fine. Not far down, the beans were mouldy. I didn't dig any deeper. If some of the beans were mouldy they all had to go. I certainly was not going to pick through them again.

That tub of beans represented hundreds of hours of work. Dad had bumper crops and no market. He rigged that old tub, probably forty years ago, as a place to store his harvest. Boxes were placed on top, and before long, he never thought about them again.

He planted more beans each year, while keeping at least 150 pounds in his damp basement.

Dad became suspicious whenever I focused on a project. The stir of activity in the cold room had him on high alert. He worries that I am going to throw something away. When he was growing up, nothing was ever discarded. Every can and jar and piece of string might have a future use. He still has that mindset.

"What are you going to do with those?" he asked, when he saw me coming up from the basement with the first of many buckets of beans.

"Compost heap."

"Nothing wrong with those beans," he said.

"Look at them," I said. "They're mouldy."

He picked up a handful and let the beans dribble through his papery fingers back into the bucket. "Not all of them," he said.

"I'm not picking through them," I said. "These beans are forty years old and they're rotting. I want them out of the house. The place stinks."

"What a shame," he said. "Perfectly good beans."

At this same time there was a good-sized cardboard box of Jacob's Cattle beans on a shelf in the garage. These beans were only about five or ten years old, and there was enough to feed a bean-eating family for years. Dad never remembers these beans exist. Several times, when he was still planting in the main garden, he'd start talking about how many rows of beans he should grow.

I said, "Let's use up the ones we have first. No need to plant any more."

"Where do we have any beans?" he asked. "We don't have any beans."

I'd remind him of the box in the garage, but directly below his living room chair, in that very same corner of the house in the cold room, sat a washing machine tub full of beans that we all had forgotten about.

Hundreds of hours of child labour spent filling that tub of beans in the basement cold room. Still more work decades later lugging the beans back outside and dumping them. Once the tub was light enough, my brother helped carry the whole damn thing upstairs and out the door. Dad hated the sight of me throwing out his good beans. I hated the thought of all the hours of my youth wasted on those beans, just to have them languish in the basement.

During my teens, I was considered lazy because I'd rather read classics of world literature than do real work. In one memorable episode, in the midst of plowing through the relentless heft of *The Brothers Karamazov* instead of mowing the lawn, my mother told me, "You're so lazy, you stink."

Each bucket of beans I lugged out of the basement cold room had more than a physical weight. Each represented a lost opportunity.

For my own bitter amusement, I started naming the buckets as I carried them out. These two were Crime and Punishment. The next two were Pride and Prejudice. Four especially heavy buckets were designated War and Peace, books one and two. The beans were *The Plague*, I was *The Idiot*, and the jars of toxic preserves lined up on the bare wooden shelves spoke to me of *Cannery Row*.

So much waste all around. Still more time spent justifying my actions to Dad, over and over, every time he brought it up. Finally, he once again forgot all about the washing machine tub of beans in the basement and never mentioned it again.

———

THE FRUIT FLIES, THOUGH. That is another story.

What might that story be?

Once the flies are gone, and I am gone, the events settle in Dad's mind.

On my next trip to visit my father this is what he said to me: "Don't know what you did, but last time you came home we had fruit flies something fierce. I had a heck of a time getting rid of them. I don't want to go through that again. So be careful how you do things."

6

CRABBY OLD MAN

I am well aware that one can't get along without domineering or being served. Every man needs slaves as he needs fresh air. Commanding is breathing—you agree with me? ... The essential thing, after all, is being able to get angry with someone who has no right to talk back. "One doesn't talk back to one's father"— you know the expression? In one way it is very odd.

—Albert Camus, *The Fall*

WHEN I WAS MUCH YOUNGER I had this plan for my parents. My mother would take care of my father until he died. He was older than she was, plus women live longer. He was bound to die first, by my reckoning, and my widowed mother would live on. She would live with me in my big house. Maybe she'd have her own wing. I imagined we would be close but separate. Imagine that—I thought we would be separate. We would live together, but not really.

I had the future all planned.

But the present, when it comes, pays no attention to the future you imagined in the past.

Dad is now ninety-four. Even if Mom had not died in the car accident, he probably would have outlived her by now.

I never expected to help care for my father in his old age. I really do take after Dad—he never made plans for his old age, either.

Only recently (that is—fifteen or twenty years too late) did he conceive the notion of selling his house. Dad called his insurance broker to cash in his life insurance. He wanted to raise some money, buy something smaller, live all on one floor. "No more stairs," Dad said. "That's what I want. I'd never build another split-level!"

My brother phones in a panic. If Dad cashes in his insurance and creates taxable income his government benefits, which are means-tested, will disappear. Support from Veterans Affairs is also contingent on my father living with my brother, because the care plan is based on their assessment that Dad is not capable of living on his own.

I call Dad to talk about tax planning. When he sold the land across the road for the new fire hall, he had to pay capital gains tax, and lost what he calls his pension for a year. He never stops talking about the whack of income tax he had to pay when he sold the land to the town. I'll just remind him how decisions can have tax consequences, and urge him to look at the big picture.

"If you lose the support from Veterans Affairs," I say, "you'd have to pay for services yourself."

"That's okay," he says. "I can do without."

My memory is so wonky—I keep forgetting Dad lives in a world where he does not really need any help. He believes he is independent. Just because he has help does not make him any less independent.

Luckily, my brother has a power of attorney that my father set up several years earlier—actually, at the same time he sold the land. Dad's lawyer suggested one be in place, just in case, and Dad said yes, that's a good idea. Dad did this all on his own. Didn't even tell my brother he had done it.

The insurance broker talks to my brother and they decide to wait. Dad can get a bee in his bonnet, but in a few days the commotion passes and all is forgotten, as if it never happened.

I can't imagine my father selling his house. He has not moved in forty-five years—does he have any idea how much work it would be to clean out every room, every closet, the attic, the basement, the sheds, go through everything, and move? Handle and move absolutely everything. Dad became bitterly distressed when my brother attempted, under Dad's close supervision, to sort through a small fraction of the junk piled in the garage. Just tackling the garage, just one room, was a nightmare. Dad struggled to agree to let anything go and resented being pressured. In order to downsize, he'd have to part with most of his stuff, which would be great—but realistically I cannot see how this could happen.

Inertia will not allow my father to move.

———

DAD HAS A SPECIAL TASK he saved just for me. He can't wait to tell me about it.

"I'm glad you're here," he says as soon as I walk through the door, suitcase still in my hand. "I have something for you to do."

When my father comes up with a chore for me, it is always manual labour. I am still, in his eyes, little more than a work machine. On another visit, Dad wanted me to cut brush. When I suggested hiring teenagers and offered to pay for it myself, Dad said, "Oh no, it's too hard and dirty for teenagers." It was never "too hard and dirty" when I was an actual teenager, and remarkably Dad still considers cutting brush a good job for George to do when he gets home.

"Teenagers are different now," Dad explained to me, as if I had just woken up on this planet and required basic orientation. *Yes, Dad, and I am different now, too. Haven't you noticed? I'm a middle-aged office worker.*

Now that I openly decline the more strenuous chores, I feel he sees me as even more useless.

The summer was dry, and Dad's peanuts in the garden across the driveway suffered. Dad was staggering around in the heat with a watering can, sprinkling his pet peanut plants and ignoring the thirsty pole beans and broccoli.

So now Dad wants me to dig a trench through the lawn and across a packed-down path used by my brother's tractors. He intends to lay a pipe in this trench and along the hedge at the end of the driveway so he can water the garden.

Have you ever used a shovel to dig a thirty-foot trench through sod? My father seriously thinks, *George will do it!* This is the kind of real work I loathed when I was younger. Now I refuse. One of the most important things I have learned is that a simple "No" can prevent a lifetime of resentment.

I tell Dad I have back problems and will not be digging a trench.

"I'll have to do it myself then," Dad says.

"Okay," I say, calling his bluff.

On a reel attached to the side of the house a garden hose is coiled, waiting. This hose is how we used to water the garden across the driveway—and when I say it's how we used to water the garden, I mean it is how people other than Dad used to water the garden. Dad just told people what to do.

Dad intends to attach the buried pipe to the outdoor tap where the garden hose already is. He looks at me like I'm nuts when I suggest using the hose instead of digging a trench across the lawn.

Dad says if I dig the trench, he'll do the rest. He could never have bent over and worked that hard.

To top it all off, my brother has a cute little miniature backhoe with a ten-inch bucket attachment perfect for digging a pipe trench. With the backhoe, it's a twenty-minute job. My brother never even heard about this scheme to run a water pipe through the lawn to irrigate four peanut plants until I told him what Dad wanted me to do on my vacation.

Yes, Dad saved this special chore just for me, and for me alone.

And now he takes a run at being disappointed in me because I continue to refuse to help him, each time he tries his luck and brings it up again.

"Use the garden hose," I say. "That's what it's there for. It's a lot easier than digging a trench."

"It's not easier for me," he says. "Dragging on that hose."

"It's easier than digging a trench," I say. "And that's what's important. It's easier for me."

"I see," he says. He seems amused.

"Okay, then." He fake huffs, then has to chuckle.

———

WHEN I VISIT MY FATHER I watch a lot of television—and by a lot, I mean way less than the average North American adult. In my own life I don't watch much television. I don't own a television, or have cable, or even have the internet at home (except on my phone).

Tennis Channel is my backup station, and I check out programs on history, animals, and weirdness. Bookmarked into the rotation are *Ancient Aliens* (on the Hitler channel), *Intervention*, and anything to do with obsessions and addictions.

The ads are grating, and depressing. American ads are all drugs drugs drugs and sick sick sick. I do my damnedest to flip around to avoid learning what people are saying about the latest gizmo to check your glucose level or to improve circulation. I begin to worry that I, too, have restless leg syndrome—except I have it in my thumb. All that flicking around reveals a number of class-action lawsuits, many against drug companies. There is a whole industry devoted to being sick and selling drugs, and they make money coming and going. If the drugs turn out to be dangerous, there is still more money to be made. The sheer breadth and depth of the scheme is the genius of late-stage capitalism.

My television collage looks something like this: Two minutes of the world's cutest kittens on Animal Planet, three minutes of hidden pyramids ("Could they have been built with the help of advanced extraterrestrial technology? Ancient astronaut theorists say yes"), one minute of "Your drug abuse affects me in the following ways."

Antiques Roadshow is always good for a linger.

There is a perverse pleasure watching compulsive hoarding shows with my father. But Dad never sees himself in these cluttered messes. He has trouble following the plot because there are at least two storylines and he cannot tell them apart. Clips from upcoming episodes also confuse him. The world is edited much too fast for him now.

At the same time, I'm skipping from *Hoarders* to *Animal Cops: Houston*, then to a vintage Borg–McEnroe tennis showdown. Do you think my restless thumb syndrome might contribute to Dad's confusion?

The real reason I watch *Hoarding: Buried Alive* is this: When I return to my apartment in Vancouver I will be able to think, *Hey, this isn't so bad.*

———

THE NESTED STACKS OF PLASTIC CONTAINERS stored on top of the fridge are too brittle to even pick up. My father permits me to put them into recycling.

Tidying up around my father requires stealth. I have to sneak around just to accomplish a mundane chore. It's best to wait until he is napping or out of the house. If he sees me leaving the kitchen with an empty can or jar, he will be concerned.

"Where are you going with that?"

"Blue bin."

"All right." He is reluctant to give his consent, but he knows I will argue about this. I will resort to simply stating what I am doing: "I am putting this in the blue bin."

Dad does not trust me with an old jar or a scrap of paper. He does not trust that I will know whether something is garbage or recycling. He wants every tiny little decision run past him; otherwise, he gets upset.

On earlier trips, before care workers were on the scene, I spent hours cleaning. I had my little projects. One mission was to clean off the dining room table so that my father, my brother, and I could all sit there at the same time. Except for two little islands of space where my father and brother each ate (never at the same time), the table was cluttered with medication, grocery store flyers, junk mail, scissors, garbage, important papers, cotton balls from pill bottles, twist ties, crumbs, and bread bags.

Bread bags?

Yes, well, that was Dad's system.

He kept a plastic bread bag on the table and used that to store other bread bags. When he finished a loaf of bread, he reached over and tucked the bag into his collection of bread bags. Neat, yes? There is a certain satisfying symmetry here—bread bags stored inside a bread bag. But these bags accumulated for months. Besides being dirty, they were in the way. I suggested the collection of plastic bread bags go into the recycling bin. You cannot believe how much we talked about this momentous issue.

"Where will I put my empty bread bags?" Dad wanted to know.

"Into the recycling."

"But that is not convenient."

"Put it over by the dishwasher and someone will take it down with other things."

He was not convinced, but sometimes I have to put my foot down. "Dad, they're full of crumbs and attracting bugs. I'm trying to clean off the table so we can all sit down and eat together. Maybe we'll even have company, so the whole table needs to be cleaned off. The dining room table is for food. It's not the place to store garbage."

Once the table was cleared off, and wiped down, the old Formica tabletop was actually a much lighter shade of dirty brown. The dining room felt more open and inviting. Dad's necessary items (scissors for his wheatgrass ritual, pill bottles) are gathered into a large metal biscuit tin that is moved to the counter during meals, and then returned to the table.

And so it went. The three of us did start eating together. We even had a guest on a holiday, so four of us sat down to a Thanksgiving meal at the freshly liberated dining room table.

My father has his place at the end of the table. My brother also has his place. The table is usually pushed up against the wall, so the other end, my old spot, is unavailable. I sat in my mother's place.

Dad always sits in his place, but sometimes my brother and I switch places.

———

WHEN I COME HOME NOW the cleaning is all taken care of, but there are always other chores. Angela wanted a clothesline put up, and it was hard to find one long enough. We're also in the process of emptying out Dad's old den in case we need to move his bedroom to the main floor.

In the den one day, my brother and I are sifting through my brother's junk, which is piled on top of Dad's junk. We hear the scuff of Dad's sheepskin booties coming down the hall. He stands in the doorway, glaring at me.

"Get—the—hell—out." He fiercely enunciates each word, and then scuffs back to the living room.

My brother and I look at each other.

"What was that about?" I ask.

My brother shrugs. "Who knows."

I head into the living room to take the bull by the horns.

"Dad, are you upset about something?"

Of course, he is concerned I am throwing away everything that is important and meaningful. I talk to him about the purpose behind cleaning up the den, and show him what I deem to be disposable (business receipts and invoices from the 1970s). I remind him that all of his more recent financial documents (covering about fifteen years) are safe in the living room in that grey box next to the fireplace. That grey box was created as a repository years ago when I attempted, with Dad, to go through piles of paper and condense everything important into one spot.

Every time I visit now, after Dad heads off to bed I go through the fresh stacks of mail—mostly pure junk hiding something important and forgotten. Each spring I get Dad organized and take him to the accountant to prepare his income tax. I know more about his sources of income and his assets than he does, but he acts like I'm throwing his "system" out of whack. He talks about his system as something infallible, but as far as I can tell it means keeping everything forever but not being able to find anything. But now, when he can't find something, he has someone to blame—George has been monkeying with his system.

I drag out the grey box and show him how everything remotely important is organized, all in one place. Finally, he cools off from his tantrum and then it is time to think about dinner.

Needless to say, no work gets done in the den.

———

ANGELA AND HER TEAM TRANSFORM THE HOUSE. It is fresher, cleaner, and feels like a home again. She cooks for my father and my brother, and they eat together. They don't talk much, but Angela and my brother talk, and Dad mostly listens. Life is going on around him and I hope he feels involved. He's certainly eating better and no longer as socially isolated. He basks in the warm glow of attention and does not mind at all having his whims catered to—by the girls.

More and more, Dad just points at things. Something he wants, something he wants taken care of. He points a finger and people start guessing. It's like a game of charades, but I don't play by the rules. "Use your words," I tell Dad. "What do you want?" Sometimes he'll just point a little harder, as if that will help me read his mind. Usually it's perfectly obvious what he wants, but my sarcasm has a purpose. It's use it or lose it when you are ninety-four, so I might be deluding myself but I hope I'm helping his brain by encouraging him to talk. Otherwise his words might drift even further away, and end up permanently just out of reach.

Of course there's a bit more to it than that. Dad's care workers are so accommodating that now Dad expects everyone to anticipate his needs and jump at every request—even the unspoken ones. I feel Dad should contribute a tiny bit more, even if it is merely by saying what he wants.

My brother is running for town councillor, so on top of everything else there is an election campaign to run. I help answer emails from voters seeking my brother's position on topics of concern. I'm considered to have the ability to blather on convincingly without ever really saying anything.

So at least I have one discernible talent.

At dinnertime, Dad asks my brother who to vote for and they discuss the candidates. Angela tells me this is the longest conversation she has ever seen my father and brother have.

Later, I take my father up town to the polling booth. He seems mildly offended that he has to show identification. He just assumes that everyone knows who he is, and they do, but rules are rules.

"What next," he says, with a chuckle.

Presumably, my father votes for my brother.

On our way back to the house Dad tells me something revealing. He says, "I was never a town councillor."

This is the first I'd heard of this. "Did you ever run?" I ask.

"No," he says.

"Did you want to run?"

"No," he says, a little annoyed now with my probing questions. His statement that he was never a councillor feels odd. If it was never Dad's ambition to be on the town council, or run for office, why is he musing out loud about it? My father is weirdly competitive with my brother.

My brother's life is taking him in new directions, and Dad makes the story about him. The story could not simply be: *Great, my son is running for town council.* Instead, Dad's story becomes: *I was never a town councillor.*

My father has mentioned something else to me several times. He comments on my brother's health and says, "I might live longer than he does."

I find it all very strange. Sometimes I wonder if that is my father's goal, to outlive my brother. If that is what is keeping him alive.

————

Do you want to hear a long story about cans of mushrooms? I know right? Canned mushrooms are too often completely overlooked in these narratives.

According to legend, these dented cans of sliced mushrooms dated from my mother's era—pre-1980, probably. My general policy in my father's house is to discard food items when they are more than ten years past their best before date. Before ten years is controversial, and not worth the battle. More than ten years gives me ammunition.

I can't find a date on these cans—either they are from a time before cans were stamped, or the dates have been lost to corrosion.

Canned mushrooms *at their best* are slimy and disgusting. I don't know why anyone would buy them in the first place. But my parents were like that with food. Dad is still like that—he'll buy something on sale he doesn't even want just because it is so cheap.

The mushrooms were cheap because the cans were dented. Dented cans do not keep. The idea with buying dented cans on sale is to use them right away.

These dented, corroding cans of slimy sliced mushrooms had been sitting on the pantry shelf for at least thirty years. I figured it was time to get rid of them.

Dad would not hear of it.

"They might still be good," he said.

"Canned mushrooms are never good," I said. "They're slimy and disgusting."

"There's that," he agreed, and laughed.

"If you don't want to throw them away, let's donate them to the food bank. There's a collection bin up by the grocery store."

"Oh no," Dad said. "We can't give them away. They might not be safe to eat."

We stood there looking at each other, me holding a retro-looking dented can in each hand. "So, we can't throw them away because they might still be good, but we can't donate them because they might not be safe to eat."

"That's about right." Dad chuckled. Even he seemed to find it all absurd.

Dad doesn't like canned mushrooms but can't throw away what he never really wanted in the first place. And we can't give them away because he doesn't want a stranger to get sick. They might not be safe to eat, but we should keep them because they might be good—even though we don't dare eat them. And wouldn't want to eat even if they were good. Which is unlikely, after all these years, considering they started out slimy and disgusting.

These pathetic little dented cans existed in purgatory, in limbo, in their own little bardo—in the gap between one state and another. Too good to throw away, and too bad to give away. Back into the pantry they went, the little rings of corrosion imprinted on my mother's ancient shelf-liner waiting for them, marking the spot they call home.

They sat on the shelf for another year, two years, three years, until finally, in a daring unsupervised moment, I sneak the cans out of the house and into a dumpster by my brother's store. I confess—I don't even open them up to compost the contents. I just toss them, and Dad never notices because he didn't care about the mushrooms. He just did not want to authorize me to do anything with them. He couldn't bear for them to leave his zone of control.

Before the advent of Meals on Wheels and then care workers, Dad lived on the cheapest frozen meals from the grocery store. He claims he can cook, but what that means is he can microwave a Pizza Pocket or a TV dinner.

When I arrived home I could see exactly what my father had been eating because he saved all the packaging. Like a contemporary archeological site, layers of debris were found in garbage middens piled around the kitchen.

This was his routine: Dad microwaved his frozen dinner, ate his meal off the plastic tray, slipped the unwashed tray back into its cardboard box, and added the box to the teetering collection stacked high atop the microwave, the dishwasher, wherever there was room.

The sight of dozens of these stacked packages was disheartening; each empty box now carried the weight of a lonely, unhealthy meal. Besides needing to handle my father's loneliness, I had to clean up this mouldy, stinky clutter. I had to. I could not even begin to cook in a dirty kitchen.

The first time Dad saw me tackling stacks of food packaging he tried to interrupt. "Separate the plastic and the cardboard," he instructed me, "so they can be recycled."

"If you wanted to do that, Dad, you've had several months to take care of it. Dirty plastic can't go into recycling."

"They can be washed," Dad suggested.

"I'm not washing these dirty old things."

"It's easy enough to do."

Only a few hours into the visit and I was already cranky. "Well, Dad, if it's so easy, why haven't you done it? I'm taking care of it now and I'm doing it my way. If you don't like the way I'm handling it maybe you should start cleaning up after yourself."

I stacked the plastic trays and flattened the boxes, furiously pitching the whole lot into garbage bags just to get the frigging mess out of my kitchen.

Dad cannot throw things away but he will incinerate. There's a wood furnace in the basement, and Dad used it to burn garbage. Despite his ecological bent, he would burn plastic without caring about air pollution. The whole house stewed in a foul, reeking miasma when he burned garbage in the furnace.

It's the domino effect again.

Carrying a tray of peanut seeds in little pots to germinate in the tropical warmth of the little room with the oil furnace, Dad fell down the basement stairs. For safety reasons, my brother then insisted that Dad no longer make trips to the basement. You will have to imagine the blunt negotiations between these two, which culminated in the promise to rip out the wood furnace if Dad so much as touched it again.

Falling on the basement stairs was only part of it. During a power outage, Dad was feeling a chill and started a fire, forgetting that the wood furnace relies on an electric blower. My brother just happened to come home and smelt scorching metal. He rushed to rig up a generator to blow out the overheated furnace. This is the kind of mistake that ends in a house fire. So now Dad is entirely banned from the basement and especially forbidden to use the wood furnace.

He can't throw away and can no longer incinerate. Dad's garbage piles up in the house, a chore for someone else to take care of—if he lets them.

———

MY FATHER'S CONTROLLING NATURE TRIGGERS ME and I am angry before even setting foot in the house. My brother vents during the drive from the airport, and that is enough to breathe new life into the burning embers of my fiery, rebellious impulses. I steel myself for what I am heading into.

Dad is frustrated with me, too, because each time I arrive I am the proverbial new broom. I am keen to clean up and toss out. Garbage pickup is only once every two weeks, so I try to make the most of it. I'm here for about three weeks, so that usually means two garbage days. A garbage day is a special event—a chance to declutter. Every bit helps. What a nightmare to come home on one trip and discover I just missed garbage day, so there would be only one garbage event to look forward to. There is a limit, you see, to how much can be put out at once.

My father keeps a cardboard box next to his recliner chair to collect the paper recycling. I come into the living room with a recycling bag and immediately he gets pissy.

"What are you doing?" he demands.

"Taking out the recycling."

"I'll do it later."

In Dad-land these days, "later" never arrives.

"I'm just getting it ready," I say. "Needs to go out tonight or first thing in the morning."

He cools off a bit, or I just ignore him and start emptying the the box. It is mostly the daily paper (the *Chronicle Herald*), as well as flyers and junk mail. But there are also chewed-on apple skins thrown in there, and farther down, a quicksilver glimpse of shoals of fish darting in the depths. Silverfish amuse me; they are not nearly as creepy as cockroaches, and I admire their lively tenacity. They are tiny animated fossils sprung to life, surviving unchanged for millions of years. I imagine they have a good life in my father's cardboard box, dining on dust and masticated apple skins, performing their elaborate mating rituals in a newsprint castle on checkerboard dance floors of discarded crossword puzzles.

I now have my eye on that dirty old cardboard box next to my father's chair in the living room—the equivalent of the bread bag full of bread bags on the dining room table. It may seem convenient, but it is ugly and unsanitary. When I emptied that box, and saw the apple skins and silverfish, I knew it was simply a matter of time before the box followed its contents out the door.

Maybe that is why Dad did not want me to touch the recycling. All too often, when I get too near, I decide certain changes have to be made.

I am definitely a mixed blessing.

If indeed I am a blessing at all.

———

MY ANGER AND FRUSTRATION flow through the house in waves, sweeping clean here, turning a blind eye there. I often think of one scene, years ago, as the prototype for all my subsequent attempts to restore or impose order. This historic scene may be an emotional template, but since then I have managed to tone down the volume.

I was home on a visit—probably in the early 1990s. My mother had been dead for a few years, but I had not grown used to the house in her absence.

Fed up with the slovenly disorder, I decided to do a bit of cleaning. Marching around the house with a garbage bag, I picked up stuff that was obviously trash—much as one might pick up litter. The floor in my father's bedroom was strewn with cardboard from shirt packages, plastic wrappers, and other debris.

When I came down into the living room, Dad was all wound up.

"What were you doing in my room?"

"Collecting garbage off the floor."

"How would you like it," he said, "if I came to your place and threw your stuff away?"

"This is what I'm collecting." I was insulted that I had to show Dad the pieces of garbage I had dared to volunteer to pick up off his bedroom floor.

"Still," Dad said, his bluster undiminished. "Might be something I wanted."

Already frustrated by the mess and the chaos, I erupted into a full-blown tantrum.

"Do you want to keep this then?" I tossed a plastic wrapper and a piece of stiff white cardboard onto the living room floor. "Do you want this? Or this?" I pulled all of his garbage out of the bag and threw it down on the dirty carpet.

I stormed out of the house and walked as far as I could get and still be on our land, down to the far end of the big garden by the river. I was boiling over, with anger and grief, and resented that my good intentions were not appreciated. I had a good cry, emptying myself of the seething inchoate turmoil.

When I wiped my tears away and took a deep breath, there was one thing I knew beyond any doubt.

I missed my mother.

I missed my mother so much I was stepping right into her shoes and acting just like her.

The garbage I had picked up in my father's bedroom and thrown down in the living room stayed there until I could stand it no longer. Eventually, I picked it all up again and threw it away. Otherwise, Dad would have just clomped over it for years in his dirty old boots.

My father's house is trigger-land, and trying to clean or do anything else is always a complicated process: one part diplomacy, one part duplicity, and three parts elbow grease.

No wonder I cannot help but turn into a crabby old man.

———

MY FATHER GOES TO BED and then I can eat in secret. Watching TV and eating is a marvellous combination, but to watch TV and eat while alone is to be truly alive.

I can eat ice cream in Nova Scotia, ice cream by the gallon.

Several little bowlfuls, one after another, in a silent communion with my mother.

Mom loved her endless little bowls of ice cream. Each bowl was "one last one."

Ice cream is an addiction. It should really be called vice cream. There is a vegan product called Rice Dream. The whole frozen treats aisle really is a vice dream.

Most often, I am addicted to salty crunchy things. Potato chips, especially. Salty, fatty, crunchy things are a particularly vivid and tactile vice dream.

Eating alone and watching TV and stuffing my feelings.

It's not like I feel sad at these moments, even though my father's future is staggering towards me and I'm going to have to wrestle with it, whatever it turns out to be, when it falls into my arms.

I don't feel sad because I don't feel anything at all. Remote control in one hand, the other free to feed chips into my mouth. Everything is swallowed. There is no room for feelings. This is not emotional eating because there are no emotions. There is no space to be anything but distracted. And visiting Dad these days, I need a lot of distraction.

My brother and I talk about being the adults now, in relation to our father, but we are adults with short fuses, struggling to cope with a father who never wants to cede an inch of territory.

It is hard to be fifty years old and treated like children by a parent whose welfare consumes our time, energy, and money.

Much like those cans of mushrooms, Dad occupies a hazy zone, an in-between state. He is post-adult, entering his second childhood, and neither competent nor incompetent. Legally, he is still considered competent (having never been through the process and declared otherwise), but everyone around him accepts that he needs some help. We try to help, and he pushes us back every step of the way.

Everything we try to do, he makes harder.

The recipe for help is much the same as the approach to cleaning—an admixture of diplomacy, flattery, duplicity, patience, belligerence, and endurance.

Mostly endurance. Emphasis on endure.

———

SPENDING TIME AS AN ADULT WITH MY FATHER helps me to reconnect with my deep well of crippling shame. There was a time when I believed my crippling shame was a thing of the past, but oh no, it feels like it never left. It's like a bout of chicken pox that was active during childhood but then buries itself in the body, waiting to resurrect as shingles.

This is what I have now. The shame equivalent of shingles, a painful outbreak that usually attacks older people during times of stress.

There are stories that make me cringe as soon as Dad launches into them. And I'm not just talking about peanuts. His repertoire is more than peanuts. Why does it matter to me what people think of my father? Do I assume they are judging him and therefore judging me? Why are my father's quirks and obsessions so mortifyingly humiliating?

Dad does not remember falling down the basement stairs carrying a tray of peanuts. He does not remember being so shook up after this tumble that he went to the bathroom and then could not get back up off the toilet. He does not recall phoning a neighbour to come help him. He does not remember falling down the stairs to the garage only a day or two later. In both cases he flew face first onto a concrete floor. Yet, miraculously, his injuries were minor. He did twist an ankle, and that was when we got the lift chair. The lift chair looks exactly like his old La-Z-Boy recliner, with the added feature of coming forward and rising up to help him stand without struggling to find his balance.

Dad fastidiously declines to ever use the lift assist feature. If he goes even an inch too far bringing the chair forward, he fiddles with the control to ensure the chair is at what he deems to be "neutral" before attempting to stand. He is that determined to resist any bit of assistance.

Dad denies falling on the ice in the driveway.

He does not remember falling near his greenhouse, and my brother getting him back on his feet with the aid of an old tractor tire that was to be used as a cold frame.

He does not remember ever falling, except for one time in the bathtub, and he asserts that was not even really a fall because he did not hurt himself.

The story of how he fell in the bathtub is the only falling story he ever tells. It is a story I have heard innumerable times, and I always wonder what is going through the mind of the listener as Dad tells this tale.

"I went down in three stages," Dad says, rather formally, making it sound more like elaborate choreography than an accident.

He was standing in the bathtub showering and then—well, he "went down." However, the cleverness of the "three stages" strategy was that it precluded injury. One is led to believe that this experience was an exercise in ingenuity more than an accident in the bathroom.

"Then I was down in the tub," Dad continues, "and I thought, what am I going to do now? So I reached over and grabbed the toilet and pulled myself back up."

And that is the gist of Dad's "three stages" falling story.

I try to re-create the scene as my father described it. I stand in the tub but skip the falling in three stages component. That might be a crucial element but without a movement coach I doubt I could do it justice. Sitting in the tub, I reach toward the toilet and discover my arms need to be six feet long. It is impossible to sit in the tub and reach the toilet. It had to have happened a different way, but Dad's telling of the story has worn a groove in his brain, and that groove is the only track this story runs on. There is no other version.

This version is Dad's truth, and I feel ridiculous amounts of shame whenever he tells his falling in three stages story to an occupational therapist, a new care worker, his doctor.

It is so obviously false, and my boundaries are such that it makes me obviously false as well.

My deep well of shame never runs dry.

The vastness of my shame is indeed a renewable resource.

———

THIS IS MY SEVENTH TRIP TO SEE DAD in three years. Sometimes I ask myself why I have taken this on. I've suddenly become the dutiful son after many years of mutual neglect.

When I came in 2010 (on what I call the "first trip"), I could see Dad needed me. He was ninety-one, floundering, and discouraged. "This is not living," he told me.

The hero child saw an opportunity. Even if Dad does not admit he needs help, the hero child feels the attraction of need. The hero child needs someone to rescue, needs to be needed. Caretaking gives me more of a defined role in relation to my father. It has given me an identity. I'm now the son I never was before.

Yet underneath this fresh new view, there is also stagnation. It's my childhood all over again, but this time with a fierce attention.

I'm revisiting all my childhood issues, all the nostalgia and all the pain.

Dwelling again (as one does) on the sentiments and the resentiments.

Dad is a vehicle to help me see myself more clearly.

For that alone, I'm supposed to be grateful. Maybe even at times I am.

So much anger keeps surfacing that I am taken aback. As my father becomes weaker, does my anger feed on his weakness and become stronger? Instead of cultivating compassion for my elderly father and his predicament, I seethe inside with a murky brew of old resentments and fresh grievances.

Rarely is my anger aimed directly at my father. (Once in the kitchen when I was venting he did turn to me and say, "Are you done?") My anger is expressed much less often than Dad's anger. His flows more freely, encouraged perhaps by being largely ignored. But still I am pissed enough to ask: Why is my father allowed to be angry and I am not?

The answer is found in my father's situation—so much has slipped out of his control. All he has left is anger. Impotent anger.

When my mother was still alive, I was more sympathetic to my father. I saw him as bullied and silenced. After my mother died, my father's personality blossomed unchecked, and then I had to deal with him directly, without an ally, without my mother as intermediary. I no longer had two parents to play off against each other. There was only Dad. And so I met Dad head-on. I met his obsessions, his stubborn refusal to talk, his inability to give an inch when challenged. I met his disinterest towards me, without my mother there to bridge the distance and pave over the gaps. I met a lack of phone calls. I met my real father, at his distance, without the counterbalance of my mother's overpowering love.

———

DURING THE SUMMER, a man starts living on the street in my hometown and causes a sensation. Television journalists come out from Halifax and CBC does a human-interest news story: "Homeless Man in Berwick Becomes Talk of the Town."

There has never been a homeless person in this small town before. He is quite the spectacle, panhandling on the sidewalk next to the bank and Tim Hortons, sleeping in plain sight on the main drag through town. Some people think it is disgraceful; others are more sympathetic. People have been asking all summer, "What can we do about Harley?" Known to social service agencies, he is considered "hard to house." Suspicious of help, he worries people are trying to lock him up. Given a place to live where he is free to come and go, he goes. This is how he proves his freedom.

The homeless man wants to be left alone, and barks at the television crew. The human-interest element of the story is not the homeless man, but how people in the small town are reacting to him.

My brother announced the news to me during a phone call. "We have a homeless person now," he said, much as one might say, "We have a traffic light now on Commercial Street." It's such a contrast to big-city life in Canada, where a homeless person is no more extraordinary than a pigeon. Homeless people are part of the landscape in Vancouver, hundreds line the cobblestone alleys, and in a shocking way they are invisible because there are so many.

The way this small town reacts to their one and only homeless person is refreshing. They have not entirely given up on each other. The small-town view is that a homeless person must be an individual in need of help.

Now it's October, and Harley is sleeping at the bus stop. There's only the one bus stop in town, and our one homeless person is there every night. The nights are getting cold, and he's made a rough nest for himself with straw pilfered from a grocery store's harvest display.

I'm in the house with my father and a care worker, starting on supper, when my brother telephones me. He's in the house, too, but downstairs in the basement rec room. I run down to see him. He's in rough shape, shivering like crazy, says he can't get warm. I touch his forehead.

He's burning up.

He wants to see Lois, the naturopath, so I call her and she says to bring him right up. Meanwhile, there has just been a car accident at the corner, so my brother insists I drive the van past the garden and straight across the field to Main Street and then go up Foster Street.

Lois takes my brother's temperature and says, "Take him to Emergency." My brother previously had cellulitis in his leg—an infection—and it seems to be back.

"Do you know what day it is?" my brother asks, chattering in the passenger seat of the van, shaking with fever.

"Yes," I say.

It's our mother's birthday. And we are on our way to Emergency.

My brother and I both remember our mother's birthday, but Dad never did, not when she was alive, and not even now that she is the undisputed love of his life.

In the bustling emergency room, my brother waits, trembling under a blanket. His phone battery has died, so I'm in charge of sending messages and combatting a barrage of rumours. Somehow the story has spread that my brother was injured in the accident that occurred at the corner just before we left the house and took off across the field.

My brother's fever is high enough that he is seen ahead of the young woman who was mowing the lawn in flip-flops, and ahead of the young man whose hand, roughly bandaged, drips bright, fresh blood on the waiting room floor. "Trailer hitch," he says sheepishly, and we all grimace in sympathy. The best thing about an emergency room in Nova Scotia is that everyone makes friends while they are waiting.

The worst thing about emergency rooms is that time is marked by hours. They put my brother on intravenous antibiotics and we are there about six hours. Six hours is judged to be "not that bad." The doctor decides my brother can return home, but will need to come in daily for more IV antibiotics. The same thing happened when his leg was infected the first time. My brother takes it all in stride.

Later that same night, in a notorious episode that makes the national news, a couple of strung-out drug dealers pour gasoline over Berwick's one homeless person as he sleeps in his straw nest at the bus stop and set him ablaze.

Harley is killed.

The next day the centre of town is all blocked off with yellow tape.

Overnight, my hometown's main drag has become a major crime scene. Rumours are flying, no one has been arrested, and everyone is wondering who on earth would do such a thing.

And all those people who said things like, "Something must be done about the homeless guy, he's an eyesore," wake up and reconsider the weight of their words. Something was done, and we are all in shock.

———

IMPORTANT UPDATE FROM THE OUTSIDE WORLD.

This last trip to Nova Scotia follows me back to Vancouver and eats at me.

Eldercare is a challenge, but on this last trip, it was my brother I took to Emergency. My brother is the person who makes my six-weeks-a-year, bi-coastal version of eldercare even possible.

And the brutal murder of the homeless man has me questioning the depth of the veneer of down-home sincerity. Does all that friendliness mask a deep, festering rot? Does raging intolerance simmer beneath the surface, ready to flare up in a heated moment?

I am triggered, and triggered hard.

I think about my mother's sudden death, and how I am now the same age she was when she died. And I dwell obsessively on all those people who have felt free to ask me why, why, why my sister took her life.

Under stress and pressure, the inside and outside worlds collide. Inside and outside jams up against each other, like tectonic plates, one sliding under compressed and stressed, and the other jutting up, ragged, raw, and fragmenting. It's true what they say. Gravity is all the more powerful when worlds overlap.

I stumble across a quote from the artist Frida Kahlo, who faced much adversity: "To build a wall around your suffering is to risk that it'll eat you up from the inside out."

Pressure. Stress. Upheaval. Walls crumble into building blocks. The result is a new mountain range of micro-memoir, called "Bingo and Black Ice."

In the spring, I don't go to Nova Scotia.

I feel guilty for being so far away and having the luxury not to go. I don't decide not to go; I just never make the plan. I'm too anxious and cannot imagine flying, which even at the best of times is completely nerve-racking. I stay in Vancouver and write about my mother's funeral. Right now, this is the most important thing in my life. It is what I am clinging to the tightest.

―――

BINGO AND BLACK ICE

THE AMBULANCE DRIVER

One of my brother's jobs was as an on-call ambulance driver. The ambulance was called out to motor vehicle accidents, along with the police and the volunteer fire department, and he'd help use the Jaws of Life to free people from the wreckage.

This frosty early December evening the dispatcher called my brother, wanting the ambulance taken out to a single-car accident on the old number one highway. The phone rang a couple of times, but before my brother answered the dispatcher hung up and called another driver.

The dispatcher said later that he didn't know why he decided to call someone else. He could not recall any reason for changing his mind. All he knew was that he was glad he did. Because otherwise, my brother would have driven the ambulance to the scene of the accident where the rescue crews were extracting the lifeless body of our mother from her car.

THE WEEK BEFORE

The week before this I was in Nova Scotia to visit my family. My sister had died (as they say) "suddenly and unexpectedly," in March of the previous year and I did not go home for her funeral. After any death, following the initial crush of friends and family, casseroles and condolences, mourning becomes more private, and lonelier. I visited about a month after the funeral, and again as often as I could. My mother was lonely. Her mother had died, and then the next year her daughter. These two women were my mother's bracketing generations. She talked to them almost daily for decades and then, suddenly, they were both gone.

THE GRAVE

Every time I went home, my mother and I visited my sister's grave in the Wolfville cemetery. "No one else wants to go with me," my mother said.

The trees in the cemetery were budding bright green, or were in full leaf, or they were bare. Yellow-trumpeted daffodils nodded in the spring breeze. Marigolds and zinnias defied the summer sun. Cut flowers wilted, dried, and crumbled into dust. My sister's gravestone never changed, and offered no clues.

By this point I was angry with my sister, although I was unable to express these feelings. I was pissed off that she had done such a horrible thing. I was pissed off that she had done a horrible thing and left me to deal with our mother, who was now even more thoroughly depressed, and confused to the point of heartbreak. I was angry about the whole business. My mother's sadness made me angrier and angrier. Anger was buried deep in my body, and everything I was feeling was filtered through this pervasive bitterness. When my sister killed herself and left an ugly mess, I didn't waste any time with denial or bargaining. I headed straight to anger and got stuck there.

I don't think my mother ever got over her daughter's death. Maybe she would have, in time, but she only had twenty-one months. Twenty-one extra-miserable months until she herself died, still grieving.

THE THEORIES

Every time there is a death by suicide people try to fill in the big blank. You make all sorts of wild guesses, because that is all you can do and you have to do *something*.

There is a paradox at work here. When someone does a crazy thing, you want to believe it was somehow, on some level, logical.

My mother promoted this theory: my sister had a lump in her breast, went for tests, but then did not wait for the results.

I developed my own theory after seeing a movie several years later. I can't recall the title, but these are the highlights: a young woman, a rural setting in the 1920s or '30s, and a hysterectomy. I believe the woman kills herself and I remember sitting in the movie theatre with my partner after everyone had left and crying my eyes out. Suddenly, I felt I had some insight into my sister's predicament. My sister had suffered from some kind of growth all over every- thing inside, a fungus perhaps, and had been scraped a couple of times but the problem kept coming back. Eventually, when she was about thirty, she had a hysterectomy. This hormonal catastrophe, plus living with chronic pain, must be an emotional bombshell. The bomb exploded. That is my theory.

The problem of course is that there is no way to ever know. The ongoing problem, when a family member kills herself, is getting used to the idea that you will never know.

Here is what I do know. In photographs, my sister is smiling and always looked happy. When I see one of these pictures now she looks like she is in pain. Her eyes look incredibly sad. The smile has become a grimace, a weak stab at a brave face for the camera. That is now all I can see, the pain and sadness in those glistening eyes, and I cannot fathom how I never saw that before.

THE WEEK BEFORE—DAD

Dad never changes, and lives on his own timeless plateau. He talked for hours and hours if Mom was not around, especially about things fifty years ago. He watches two TVs, sound and pictures, at once. He said you just focus on the one you want to watch.

When the police came to tell him his wife had died in an accident, my father said he didn't know whether to laugh or to cry.

THE WEEK BEFORE—MOM

A short round woman, Mom had taken to wearing black because black was slimming. She looked like a black ball punctuated with perky little sag-proof breasts.

We talked of death a fair amount. She was afraid, and I tried to make thoughts of death easier. She told me how as a child I used to cry when she was ill, lying down with her and saying, "Don't die Mommy, don't die."

You might think my mother had some kind of premonition. But no. She had been like that for years—imagining her absence. She was forever saying, "What would you guys do without me?"

THAT MAN

One time when I was a teenager my mother and I were shopping in town. She turned to me and said, "That man is your sister's father."

I already knew at this point my sister was born before my parents were married. I don't remember anything about the man my mother pointed out.

MY MOTHER'S STORY

Before my mother was born, her mother was a maid for a wealthy family in town. The old man of the family knocked her up, and so of course my grandmother was fired. There was no such thing as sexual harassment or sexual assault in the early 1930s. If a wealthy old man wanted something, he took it. So my grandmother was pregnant and out of a job, and this is where my mother came from. She was the unacknowledged bastard child of one of the town's most prominent and respected families.

Scorned at birth, my mother in turn rejected the hypocrites, dismissing the townspeople as pretentious snobs who "wouldn't say shit if they had a mouthful."

LUCKY TROLLS

If Dante had lived in small-town Nova Scotia in the 1980s, he could have based his vision of Purgatory on smoke-filled bingo halls crowded with doomed souls forever suspended in the state between Winning and Losing.

These doomed souls played every night (Saturday at the Lions Club in Kingston, Sunday at the fire hall in Berwick, Monday in Aylesford, and so on) and endlessly talked about almost winning: being "set"—needing only one more number to win. These women (for they were most often women) each commanded about a half-acre of bingo cards, their territory delineated by rows of big-haired lucky trolls, stuffed toys, framed photos, cigarette lighters, ashtrays, backup daubers, snack food, coffee or pop, and rows of change.

My mother always wanted me to go with her because I was deemed lucky. My mother paid my way, and we split the winnings. She played her half-acre of cards and minded my small patch as well. I often won, but I found the suspense of almost winning so excruciating I rarely agreed to go.

It was a revelation to see my mother smoking at bingo. Officially she had quit, and indeed she had—except at bingo. Suddenly I saw why she was so keen to play every night. It got her out of the house and she could smoke in secret.

She had quit, you see, after the cancer. She had breast cancer, first in one breast and then the other, and eventually had a double mastectomy. She then had annual screenings, which she found very stressful. She had been given the idea that if she could just reach five years cancer-free, then she might have good odds of living even longer.

FATHER TOO

In fact, my father also had breast cancer, and has a huge concave scar on the right side of his torso. My father had his mastectomy the year I was born and at the time his doctor gave him only a few months to live. More than fifty years later he is still alive and cancer-free.

My mother used to joke about it, declaring that her and my father only had one tit between them. She wore little foam prosthetics, and was not shy about them. In a town where some women hid their dainties in pillowcases before hanging them outside to dry, my mother washed her little foam breasts and pinned them out on the clothesline along with everything else for the whole world to see.

When feeling particularly lighthearted and mischievous, my mother would reach down her top, pull out one of her little foam tits and throw it at my father. Later, I would fictionalize such a scene by having a character reach for both her falsies at once in a double-barrelled onslaught, described as a "surreal cross-your-heart barrage." I don't recall Mom ever throwing both her tits at once, but if the first did not get enough of a reaction, she would then hurl the second. My mother only threw her tits when she was in a good mood. She mostly flung her tits at my father.

THE RAILROAD

When I left my mother drove me to the train station in our small town. This would be the last place I saw her. It would be the last time for the train as well, since passenger service to the Valley was being cancelled. I had never taken the train from the Annapolis Valley before, but this was the last chance, so that's what I did.

My mother drove me to the soon-to-be-defunct train station and said, "Come home anytime." Little did I know that in less than a week I would return for her funeral.

When I turned to wave goodbye, I had my last glimpse of my mother. She was sitting in the car, in the driver's seat, in the exact spot where she would soon meet her death. Her hand was raised up, and pressed against the glass. She was crying.

TRAVELLING, AND THE DREAM

I was living in Montreal. It took about a day to get there on the train. I could not afford a sleeper, so it was an ordeal.

I'd only been in Montreal a couple of days when the police told me the news. I returned to Nova Scotia the next day, this time by plane. I had to borrow money to buy a ticket.

For years my parents had slept in separate rooms. The bedroom where my mother slept was known as the spare room; however, this was, to my mind, my mother's room.

At that time, I still had my own bedroom in the house, preserved like a time capsule or shrine to permanent adolescence, and this room is where I always slept. I had just slept there, the week before.

When I arrived home after my mother's sudden death, I slept in her bed. The pillowcase smelled of Noxzema underscored with the burnt metallic tang of ironed cotton. From the sheets wafted hints of baby powder and Ivory soap. I slept in my mother's bed and breathed it all in.

That night I had a dream. In the dream my mother was standing in the driveway next to her car, a new car. She was all excited because she was going on a trip. She was happy.

I found this dream very satisfying, even though at the same time it seemed to be rather obvious wish-fulfillment, a transparent attempt to put a positive spin on a tragic event. Yet this dream I had when I slept in my dead mother's bed was a great comfort to me.

When I went home for my mother's funeral, I slept in my mother's bed, and neither my father nor my brother said a word to me about it.

THE UNCLE

While I was home for the funeral, one of my mother's uncles adopted me. It is strange, but now I can't remember who this was. I guess I was in shock. Hanging out with this great-uncle is mostly what I remember from that time. He lived just up the street, with his wife, in a small house they had recently moved to. The fact is, on my mother's side, there were so many aunts and uncles and cousins, and shifting factions of in-laws and out-laws, that I never did know half of them.

The great-uncle who took me under his wing—he was curious, he said. He liked to see things for himself. He drove me all around so we could see things together. He drove me to the scene of the accident—a series of curves through a low-lying stretch of the old highway. My mother's car had flown off the road and struck a hydro pole. The damaged pole was atilt and propped up with temporary struts. The earth was cut and wounded.

Next my great-uncle and I drove to the junkyard. He explained to the man that we were looking for a particular car. My uncle said "the young fella" wanted to see it. The attendant waved us in.

We drove around the junkyard (a cemetery for machines) until we found the dirt-brown Valiant. The car was deemed to be a write-off, although it did not look that bad—until we walked around to the driver's side. The driver's door was crushed inwards. There was blood. On the bent steering wheel, on the jagged crushed door, and everywhere you looked, until you stopped looking.

The uncle, who liked to see things for himself, commented on what had happened, based on what he could divine. "She must of hit the black ice there on the curves through the marsh, and slid off the road ninety degrees into the power pole. The side of the car there, that's what hit. She flew around and hit the pole right there square on. Yes sir. That's what happened. Hit the ice there, flipped around into the pole, and that was that."

Then we went back to his house, sat in the kitchen, and drank rye. We had seen for ourselves all there was to see.

THE HYDRO POLE

The hydro pole that arrested the flight of my mother's car had to be replaced. A few months after her funeral, the power company sent my father a bill. This bill, for replacing the hydro pole damaged in the accident that killed my mother, provoked most of the emotion my father expressed following his wife's death. He was some upset. Oh, he was livid. He could not believe anyone could be so callous. In a huff, he phoned the utility—he was a shareholder, after all, not just a customer—and declared he would not pay their bill. And he did not pay. The power company declined to pursue the matter.

A VERY RECENT DREAM

The night after writing the section about my mother's uncle, I dream about my mother. We are in the kitchen of our house, near the sink, a location where I have heard many secrets. (For example, this is where we were standing when she told me she had another baby, after my sister, before she met my father. That baby was put out for adoption and remains otherwise unknown.)

In the dream, I want to ask her about the mysterious uncle who reached out to me, but I feel emotions welling up and I know that if I speak, I will cry.

My mother happens to mention Uncle Lou, who had moved to a small house up the street. How long did he live there? I ask. Four years, my mother says. So it was Uncle Lou, I thought, already starting to write the dream out in my head.

All I know for sure is that I don't ever remember seeing Uncle Lou before the week of my mother's funeral. And I've never seen him since.

THE ASHES

My mother's ashes are scattered in the garden, but nowhere near the strawberries, because she was allergic.

My father has also asked for his ashes to be scattered in the garden. He wants to be with his wife. I hope that he and my mother will not fight as much as they did when she was alive. However, my father does not remember any quarrels or tears or incessant nagging. He only remembers the good things.

THE END OF MY MOTHER'S STORY

All those years worrying about cancer and look how she died: in an instant. In a car accident. On the way home from bingo.

If I happen to mention having a dead mother, people ask, how did your mother die? I usually just say, Bingo.

What? She died playing bingo?

Well, I say, to be precise, it was a lethal combination of bingo and black ice.

And for twenty-five years I have been meaning to tell the story.

7

THE FALL

Picking: Reaching out to touch or grab unseen objects.

*Sundowning: The tendency for those suffering from
dementia to experience an increase in symptoms,
such as confusion, in later afternoon.*

IT'S FALL AND I'M BACK IN NOVA SCOTIA. I haven't seen my
father in a year, because I didn't come home in the spring.

In addition to the anxiety that is growing and threatening to
overwhelm my entire life, I had also suffered a physical injury on
my last trip. Ironically, while visiting my father, I did exactly what I
have so relentlessly warned him about.

I fell.

My ribs have healed now, but when they were still painful, and I
couldn't sleep, I fainted on the bus one morning on the way to work.
That was almost a year ago.

I had never fainted before. But I still have panic attacks at the
thought of taking public transit.

The journey to Nova Scotia starts with a short bus trip in Vancouver, then a train to the airport. Waiting; a long flight; waiting; a shorter flight. From the Halifax airport, it's an hour-and-a-half drive.

All of it more of an ordeal than usual.

Anxiety is the gift that keeps on giving.

Other than that, I'm fine.

Perfectly fine.

———

ANGELA IS STILL HERE, taking good care of Dad.

At dinner, Angela says that as soon as my visit was confirmed, my brother got right to work.

"Your postcard arrived," she says, laughing, "and the very next day he fixed the kitchen floor! I've been bugging him for weeks about that."

"He must be scared of me," I say.

"Not very likely," my brother says.

We go over the list of chores and projects to be tackled while I'm here.

"You're so lucky, Stephen," Angela says, "to have sons to look after you."

Dad looks at Angela, but does not say anything.

"They're such good sons. You're lucky to have them, aren't you, Stephen?"

Angela's prompting and cueing is usually very effective, nudging Dad in the desired direction. But this time, Dad does not budge. He will not agree that he is lucky to have good sons to look after him in his old age.

———

ANGELA GOES AWAY FOR A WEEK on vacation and I have to admit Dad goes into a decline without her.

He's all mine on Thanksgiving. I cook a full holiday meal: roast turkey breast, a bread and apple stuffing inspired by my mother's recipe, sweet potatoes from the garden, and Brussels sprouts.

After dinner, Dad starts to gag. His body convulses, like a strong hiccup, and a look of alarm spreads over his face.

I rush for the basin.

By bedtime, he's still heaving. Dry heaving, mostly. He can't really bend over, so he's trying to puke sitting up. The strain on his body looks unendurable.

He's heaving more than actually puking, but from what does come up I can see that he barely chewed his holiday meal. I think Angela cuts his food up for him more than I do.

I discuss the situation with the on-call registered nurse at the care agency. No fever? Good. Keep an eye on him, I am advised, and see how he is in the morning. If it gets worse, I should take him to the hospital.

"I don't know if he would go with me," I say.

"Then call an ambulance," the nurse says. "If you can't take him."

In the morning, Dad seems much better. A little tired, because he was up late dry heaving, but he tackles his breakfast with no problem.

And then Angela returns from her vacation. She blows through the house like a fresh summer breeze, and jollies Dad into submission.

———

FRIDAY MORNINGS DAD GOES to the adult day program. We all have to be careful not to call the day program "adult daycare," which is how it is commonly known. Certain people, my father among them, find the notion of adult daycare insulting. Dad was certainly insulted when I first suggested he might want to attend this program, as a chance to get out of the house and meet people. "That place is for people who can't stay home alone," he said.

A year or two after first mentioning it, I convinced Dad to go by pointing out that he would be doing other people a favour by being there. He would be helping people who were lonely, who didn't have anyone to talk to. "Think of the others, Dad," I said. "You can help them do the sudoku."

He is by far the oldest person in the group. When I picked him up after his first session, he was so excited, like a wound-up kid, tired from his first day of school.

"What did you do today, Dad?"

"There was a singer and we all sang."

"Singing? You were singing?"

"Yes," he said. "And lunch."

"What else?"

"Oh, we did puzzles and played games. Oh, and cake."

Having slept on it, the next day he said, "I don't think I'm going back."

He vacillated like this around his Friday program—immediate enthusiasm, and then later, a feeling of regret. It obviously improves his mood, but perhaps he feels embarrassed for being so easily entertained.

Now he confesses he'd miss the Friday program if he didn't go. It's the only place he can dance, but he is not allowed to dance with the other clients. Only with the nurses, so I think this works out rather well for Dad. The nurses who run this program are angels.

On Friday morning, he's usually ready early and waits on his stool down by the garage door. But today, Dad is still in the kitchen when the minibus pulls into the driveway. I tell Dad not to rush, to take his time—careful on the stairs!—and head out to tell the driver Dad is on his way.

In the garage, Dad is stalled trying to put on his cardigan. He has each arm in a sleeve but the whole sweater is in front of his body. He has it on backwards and keeps looking at his arms. He tugs on each sleeve, unable to figure it out. He can get an arm caught behind him, trying to get dressed, but never this.

"What in tarnation ..." he mutters.

I help him with his sweater and jacket, and then, without touching him, escort him to the minibus. Watching him walk across an open space is completely nerve-racking, like watching a drunk reel through a minefield. He appears to be constantly falling and somehow, impossibly, only just manages to keep walking. Yet he absolutely refuses the walker or his cane.

He'll be okay. The nurses at the day program will keep an eye on him.

Dad has trouble keeping his balance but will not use his cane. Certainly not in the house. Even when he used his cane outdoors, he left it down in the garage. If someone brought it up to the main floor, Dad hung it on the living room door handle and never touched it. He never took his cane with him to help him on the stairs up to his bedroom or to the bathroom at night.

Dad assures me he doesn't have to use his cane anymore. "I got better," he claims. "Don't need it."

And isn't he Mr Huffy if I dare suggest he needs it now more than ever. He invents advice to support his position: "The doctor said I shouldn't use the cane anymore."

I don't win arguments anymore, not in this new world my father has fabricated. I never win—I just stop arguing. But who even knows what winning would look like at this point.

Dad never wanted to rely on a cane because he feared he would get used to it, and then always need it. He says a crutch only makes you weaker. I have pleaded with him, back to all the old arguments, that using the cane will keep him walking and moving and doing more and doing it safely.

I can't believe we have gone so far backwards—from using the walker to arguing over the cane.

Dad is horribly unable to see himself clearly. He seems stuck in the attitude he showed at the drugstore a few years ago. We were waiting for a prescription and he said hello to an acquaintance, an elderly gent.

After the old man left, Dad turned to me. "Look at him," he said, an edge of triumph in his voice. "He's not as old as me and he has to use a cane."

Dad does not want to use a cane, and that is final.

That is the point we are at.

Again.

Friday morning is the only time I have the house to myself. It is ridiculous how much I enjoy the feeling. I do all the things I am not allowed to do with Dad in control. I turn down the heat and open windows. I throw open the curtains at the head of the stairs near my father's bedroom. (Drama continues to swirl around these calf-shit yellow curtains. The occupational therapist says they are a safety hazard. I say they are ugly and a nuisance. Dad says if they are taken down, he will move out. My brother says, "Don't tempt me.")

On Friday morning, I am free to take a shower and parade through the house in a towel, without having my father wolf-whistle at the sight of my naked flesh. He whistled at me when I was young and half-dressed, and it made my skin crawl. He never did this to my brother, only to me. Eventually, I asked him to stop, and he did. For many years, he stopped. But he has started again. I think he has simply forgotten he agreed not to do it anymore.

That it bothers me is what he enjoys, so I try not to let on.

I practise finding space to believe his whistling does not affect me. I practise acting not-triggered and practise not showing Dad that he has got to me. Denying him the joy of his teasing cackle. Taking the fun out of it, so he will lose interest.

The good shower is on the main floor in the new bathroom next to the door to the living room. It's insane how much Dad's whistling can bother me. If he is in the living room, it's all I think about while I shower. When Dad is installed in his chair, I try to zip past the living room door without attracting his attention. But on Friday morning, I can shower and roam half-naked, free as a bird. I can act like I am at home. This is really when I realize how different I have been feeling. How guarded, and armoured.

With Dad not here, I am much freer in my skin. On Friday morning, the cat's away.

The adult day program phones to say Dad is not well. I get dressed, grab his walker, and drive up to what used to be Berwick Hospital. I roll his walker into the wing with the day program. Dad seems a little out of it. The nurse says he just sat in the chair and would not talk to them.

He uses the walker to get to the van.

We drive back and get him in the house. He is meek and compliant but confused, and very tired. He beelines to his lift chair and sits there, mumbling to himself. Sometimes he points to things in the ceiling, tracing patterns in the air, or reaches for something but then seems to forget what it is he wanted. His hand lingers mid-air, like the shadow of an impulse.

"What do you see, Dad?"

"An animal in the ceiling."

"What kind of animal?"

"All white."

"Like what?"

"Like a cat."

When his care worker arrives for the supper shift she says, "I've never seen him like this."

Dad is handling the adult day program schedule printed on a thin piece of cardboard. He thinks it is a brochure. He picks at an edge, trying to open it up, then turns it over and tries the other edge. He ignores us when we try to show him it is just one piece of cardboard, not something that folds out. He keeps trying and trying.

I ask him, "Why don't you believe us?" and he says, "Why don't you believe me?"

We are both relying on the evidence of our senses. We both think, with equal force, that we are right. I know I am right, but how am I any different than Dad?

Watching him pick and pick at the edge of that cardboard, I have a flash of a horrible future: Dad in an old-age home, locked in his chair, mumbling and drooling. My fear sweeps up and out, and some tears crawl down my cheek.

Dad's care worker says, "Are you okay?" and I say yes—because, really, what else is there to be at a time like this?

Friday evening, after supper, Dad goes to the main-floor bathroom. My brother and I, talking in the dining room, are interrupted by ominous thumps and a thick thud. We look at each other and rush to the bathroom door.

"Dad, are you okay?" I ask.

He grunts yes.

Dad opens the door and hangs onto the door frame. He is wild-eyed and does not look capable of walking unassisted.

I grab his cane off the living room door handle, thinking he can use that with one hand and lean on me on the other side.

Dad glares at me with a look of complete hatred.

"Leave me alone!" he yells.

He rears back from me, shaking and agitated.

I step away from him because he is infuriated, and fed up with me.

Dad staggers into the living room. He aims for the chesterfield, but his bum catches just the edge of the cushion and he plops down to the floor.

He sits on the floor in front of the chesterfield, looking a little stunned.

This is Fall #1.

———

DAD HAS FALLEN BEFORE, of course, just as we all fall now and then. When you fall you should pause and conduct a careful inventory. Sometimes the more serious injuries are not immediately apparent. When people fall, especially seniors, it is not a good idea to move them right away.

My brother knows these things. "Leave him," he says.

I sit down across from Dad in the old platform rocker no one ever uses, and my brother settles in another chair. Dad is unable to move from where he is sitting.

"Just relax," I tell him, "until we're sure you are okay. As soon as we're sure, we'll help you up. Relax. Please just relax."

He stops struggling and calms down a little. The wild look in his eyes is like a beast inside, frantic to burst free.

"Does anything hurt?" I ask.

He shakes his head.

"I was only trying to help you," I say. It is always best to try to deflect criticism.

After a bit, he seems unhurt and relatively calm, so my brother and I each take an arm and ease him up onto the chesterfield. We all sit back down in our seats. It is time for a family conference.

This family conference is in the form of a lecture, in that I do most of the talking and Dad just sits there, enduring.

I tell him that it is necessary for his safety to follow advice and to ask for help, if he is going to be able to continue living here.

"You treat us like the enemy," I say, "but we are both trying to help you to stay in your house. That's what you want, right? We are trying to help. And if you want to stay here, you are going to have to co-operate."

My brother is probably rolling his eyes at me, but I have to believe there's still a rational creature somewhere inside our father. It's important for me to try to connect with that part of him.

My father watches me as I talk. His expression is unreadable. I wonder if any of my words are reaching him. There is a particular grunt he makes when he is being nagged with unassailable logic, a sighing, defeated "Uh-huh" sound I have heard him use a million times with my mother. This two-syllable sighing grunt means: *I hear you and yes you make perfect sense and yes I am patiently enduring you nagging at me.*

He gives me this special sighing grunt a few times until my lecture is over.

"Okay?"

One last sighing, defeated grunt.

"Can you get upstairs by yourself, or do you want some help?"

Dad does not consider this question deserves a response.

The three of us sit there in the living room for a silent moment. My brother and I start talking about other things, picking up our previous conversation, making the situation seem calm and normal.

We are entering here a season of "lasts"—although it is impossible to know this except in hindsight. This scene of us three survivors seated in the living room will be the last time we are all together in one room of this house.

Dad inches forward to the edge of the couch. He uses a rocking technique to gather enough momentum to achieve liftoff. Barely up on his feet, teetering near the corner of the red-brick fireplace, he struggles to find his balance. His stern dignity keeps his sons at a watchful distance. He gathers himself together, running on the heat of sheer stubborn pride, builds up a head of steam, and all on his own, one step at a time, hauls himself up the stairs to his bedroom.

This display of unbearable dignity will be the last time he goes up those stairs unassisted.

After a while, I pretend to need something from my room so I can glance into my father's bedroom. He's sitting on his bed, talking to himself.

"Are you tired?" I ask.

"Suppose so," he says.

"Did you take out your teeth?" (I know he has not.)

"No," he says. "Should I?"

"You always do." This kind of banter is normal for Dad, so I try not to read anything into it.

I wander off, hoping Dad will have been prompted into removing his teeth.

When I come back, he is under the covers.

"If you want," I say, "I can clean your teeth for you tonight."

He's already in bed, so it seems the least I can do.

"How would you do that?" he asks.

"Take them in the bathroom, put them in the cup, and use one of those big cleaner tablets, just like you do. C'mon," I say, "let's take out your teeth."

He loosens his lower plate with his tongue, half chokes on it, then gets it out. He holds it in his hand.

"Okay, good. Now the uppers."

He slips the lower plate back into his mouth, gags alarmingly for a heart-thumping moment, and then pulls out the uppers.

"C'mon Dad. Just give them to me and I'll clean them and you can go to sleep."

He slides the upper plate back into his mouth.

We look at each other.

"Are you going to let me clean your teeth?" I say.

"I could," he says, "but I won't."

"Okay," I say. "Good night."

I give up. I tried. I was unable to coax my father's teeth out of his mouth. To be honest, I was not keen to handle them. They give me the creeps. Dad has old dentures everywhere. Most of them belonged to people who died. They are such personal items, with their listless sheen of coral pink and yellowy white, a lingering smile half remembered but mostly forgotten. These deconstructed smiles haunt me, like cruel jokes that have lost their bite. The faces are forgotten, but the rictus smile remains—all teeth and no human warmth.

Dentures are too personal and intimate to just throw away. They have been accumulating for generations. You can't pull out a drawer in his bedroom or the bathroom without finding someone's teeth and gums just sitting there, as if waiting for a head to call home.

Later that night, I'm asleep in the spare room, on the same floor as my father's bedroom.

A godawful thumping crash wakes me. I stumble into Dad's room and he is wild-eyed on the floor at the end of the bed. Most of his bedding is on the floor with him.

"I'm okay," he says. "Don't help me."

He looks at me, standing over him lying there on his bedroom floor, and then reconsiders. "Unless you want to," he adds, like he is giving me something.

"What happened?" I say.

"I was too hot," Dad says. "I was trying to take the blanket off."

Dad is never too hot. He tripped over the bedding as he was unmaking his bed in the dark.

This is Fall #2.

He is on his back on the floor, struggling.

"Just stay there," I say. "I'll fix the bed and then help you up."

He is exhausting himself straining to sit up or roll over. I slip a pillow under his head and tell him to lie still and relax. "Save your strength."

While remaking his bed (he has it almost completely torn apart), I try to figure out if he is hurt and what is going on. His energy is strange: a troubling combination of frenzied and confused.

I have no idea how to get his 200 pounds back into bed. My brother is upstairs and needs his sleep. I decide not to wake him just yet.

I get Dad on all fours, and then ask him to rest his arms and upper body on the bed. This is when I realize that he cannot move any farther from this position.

I don't know how we do it. Somehow, using my knees and lower legs, I lever him up onto the bed.

Dad settles down on his back. His eyes stay open.

I sit on the other side of the bed and decide to linger with my father. "You're a tough old bird, aren't you?"

"What?"

"You're tough."

"Yeah."

We share a moment, the ghost of a chuckle.

"Do you want me to sit here for a while?"

"What?"

"Sit here."

"Huh?"

"Should I sit here, like this, stay a bit."

He thinks about it. "Don't take too much time," he says.

"I'm already awake."

I sit on my father's bed, hoping my company will calm him. He is under the covers, on his back, muttering to himself. He seems oblivious to my presence.

I reach out to my father's relatives. I call his parents, Evelyn and George Kenneth. I call his sister, Maxine, his only sibling who recently paved the way. I call his aunt Blanche, who never married and was always meddling. I ask his family to come help their loved one, Stephen, to come help him now, tonight, because I fear things are only going to get much, much worse.

I sit on my father's bed, praying that he will die in the night, so I don't have to take him to the hospital in the morning.

Dad gives no sign that he is aware I am still sitting with him on his bed.

His eyes roam the ceiling. His fingers reach out and grasp the air. He mutters a bit, nothing coherent, but he is not talking to me.

Every now and then, my deep, slow breathing synchronizes with his shallow huffs and puffs. Gradually, his breathing slows. But he does not sleep.

Eventually, I leave.

I remain hypervigilant, and am awake the rest of the night.

On Saturday morning Dad is up and about, rummaging in the bathroom between our two bedrooms. He is looking for something and I wonder if he even knows what. There are fifty years of poison stored in that bathroom cupboard, everything from shoe polish to animal dewormer.

Is he safe in there?

Is he going to grab a tube of ointment instead of toothpaste? No, wait. That was me. At least I noticed in time.

When today's care worker, Heather, arrives, Dad is not yet downstairs. Heather is not one of Dad's main care workers, but has been here before.

"He had a bad night," I say. "He fell twice. You may have to get him dressed and help him downstairs."

"Is he okay? What's going on?"

"Doesn't seem hurt, but he's confused. He's tearing the place apart up there looking for something but won't say what it is. Something's wrong, that's for sure. He needs to be checked out. I think the plan is to have breakfast and then take him to the hospital."

"Okay," Heather says. "We can go in my car."

While I eat breakfast, I can hear Heather and Dad talking in his bedroom. There is progress in getting him dressed.

At the head of the stairs, Dad pauses to fix the curtains behind him. Oh god—those curtains! He's turning, always a problem. He's turning and reaching, instead of holding on to the railing. He staggers—at the top of the flight of stairs, not holding on to anything.

This is Fall #3.

Tumbling like a stuntman down a flight of stairs.

No—but almost.

Heather steps up and grabs him, just as Dad is on the brink of toppling ass over teakettle down those stairs. She makes a face, like *That was close*. Dad ignores her prompt to grab the handrail and, one last time, fiddles with the curtains, making sure they are closed to his satisfaction. Fiddling with these curtains is the remedy for the feeling in his bones.

Heather takes Dad's hand to help him and he acts like she's just holding his hand.

She guides him down the stairs and makes it seem like a game.

Sometimes I'm a little jealous of Dad's care workers because he enjoys them so much. Dad accepts help from his care workers in a way he never will from my brother or me. If I try to help, Dad is insulted. He resents that I even offer. He will never accept my tenderness. He would never take my hand to walk down the stairs. With me, he just gets angry. With a woman, he becomes immediately softer, even flirtatious.

———

THERE'S A BIG COMPLICATED TOPIC that keeps coming up that I need to get off my chest.

This big topic is something we never talk about. I don't talk about it with my father and I don't talk about with my brother.

Sometimes the things we never talk about are best left unsaid.

I am careful never to be too honest with health care professionals, in case they get the wrong idea.

I have never admitted to my doctor, for example, how much I have thought about suicide. For me, suicide was a constant companion. It was a feeling I hoarded, saving it up for later. Saving the potential, keeping it with me, was like making it a companion. This is how it has been for me for as long as I can remember. But I'm careful not to reveal this too freely. My doctor worries too much as it is—and as I say, she might get the wrong idea. Suicidal thoughts are completely normal—right? In today's world? I mean, our entire culture is self-destructive and only getting worse.

I'm never going to actually do it (unless I really feel like it for some reason—I won't completely rule it out). Never is a long time and nothing lasts that long anymore. And in Canada, as of 2016, we have legalized medical assistance in dying. So that might be in my future. Always existing as a possibility.

So, where did this begin? Where did my blue eyes begin? My short-sightedness? My transient tow-headedness? It all began before time began and so has always been. Always fermenting as part of the emotional landscape, as much a fixture as anger and shame and stony silences.

I say all this for a reason. I say all this for a bit of context. I say all this so the next thing I say is not too shocking. The next thing is something even more unspeakable and something I could never admit. Friends joke about suicide, but nobody ever mentions this.

This next thing is something I have never told anyone. I write it expecting no one will see it. Writing it down feels wrong, but I do it anyway. Writing it down feels like making more of it than it ever really was.

But what was it?

I handle it, soften it, justify myself, turn it over, and imagine where I was and what was going on and what I must have been going through.

What I can never reveal, even though it is absolutely true, is that I visit my dear old dad and imagine killing him. Not *kill* him, exactly —I never thought anything like that. "Kill" is such a brutal word, and no such harshness clings to the twisted wisps flickering through my mind.

I was thinking more in terms of *being helpful*.

I would be helping him out. Helping him avoid the miseries of an old-age home. Helping him escape the ordeal of his decline, and eliminate the last miserable home stretch.

Helping him stop being so goddamn annoying and embarrassing.

Killing sounds so hard. My gentle imagining nestled in something much softer. Soft like a pillow. Soft like being put to sleep. A pillow slipped over a sleeping face to ease him out of this world and off to a better place.

I was an angel of mercy, perhaps, or an archangel. It all seems so natural and ethereal if you start talking about angels.

The angel of mercy pays a visit.

With a pillow.

Putting him down—people say that about their child, meaning getting him to settle down and go to sleep.

People also say that about their pet.

I was aiming somewhere between the two meanings, in my hazy fog of magical thinking. I would help Dad go to sleep.

And never wake up.

Every time I come home to visit my father, these notions flick past, yet somehow, at the same time, I deny the whole train of thought.

Every time I come home, what I really hope is that Dad does not die while I am here, because my guilty conscience will make me look very suspicious.

Killing myself was not ever really about me, in a strange way, but just a way to use the only weapon I had. Killing myself was a way of getting back at my parents. I used to spend a lot of time imagining how upset they would be. This idea, that they would be so upset, came in the form of a reward rather than a deterrent.

I worried about this. I actually used to worry my parents might not be totally devastated. I wanted them to find me and finally realize how precious I was. They would know they should have done more. They would be sorry. I really wanted them to be sorry.

Being worried they might not be upset enough probably saved my foolish young life.

It's normal to imagine killing your father—is it not? I mean, I used to imagine killing my mother when I was much younger and she was still alive. You know, maybe I'm just impossibly naive, but at the time I thought this was progress. To go from wanting to destroy myself to thoughts of killing a parent instead was surely a big step towards complete mental health. You see, my first impulse always was to remove myself. But then, with a bit of maturity and life experience, I began to realize the better plan might actually be to eliminate the most actively annoying of my parents.

Otherwise, obviously, I would not survive.

When overwhelmed by my mother's smothering love, I imagined means of escape. I left, as best I could, but sometimes leaving is no escape. And then she died, and I missed her. I really missed her. Although of course, as I say, she is much easier to get along with now that she is dead.

The world is a matrix of mythic structures and narratives. Patricide is what Zeus did to his father Cronus. Doesn't every son think about killing his father—in the classical mythological sense? Even in a galaxy far, far away, Kylo Ren is compelled to strike down his father, Han Solo.

Maybe in an ideal universe, a perfectly nurturing father does not have to be symbolically killed.

Maybe I'm just clearly deranged, but I have imagined killing both my parents and was suicidal since early childhood. Such is my twisted path to the present.

(Now I have probably done what I always end up doing—told you more than you ever wanted to know.)

Some people have what might be called unwanted or intrusive thoughts, where horrible ideas pop unbidden into the mind. Let's just say I must have something like that. Intrusive thoughts are tricky: if you fight unwanted thoughts, they just become worse. You can't fight it and make it go away. Rather like the dark side of the Force in the Star Wars universe—if you choose to fight it, it just gets stronger.

You can't ever really make thoughts go away. You just learn not to give them any power.

So yeah, I have had thoughts of being helpful.

But not this night.

Not the night of my father's falls.

Not at the real end. Not then.

I've always felt the impulse to destroy myself. *I've got to get out of here*, is what I say to myself. Still do today. That was how I grew up feeling. When I was young, the only way I could imagine "getting out of here" was to escape the confines of my body. I was young and lazy and a product of my environment. The easiest way to kill yourself without really doing it all at once, or taking responsibility for it, is drinking. Alcohol is a depressant and removes inhibitions. That combination is perfect for making the worst decisions. Even if by some fluke it doesn't accidentally happen all at once, heavy drinking is killing yourself on the instalment plan.

Then my sister did kill herself. Rather unexpectedly. No warnings signs, no cries for help, no half-hearted attempts.

My sister's suicide validated my own feelings, while also managing, strangely, eventually, to eliminate them. My sister's death was a fresh tragedy, and the shock, over time, reconfigured my own wounds.

The life-shattering shock inoculated me, cured me of the suicide sickness.

It was all those questions I had to ask. All those questions I was left with. Did she do everything she could before taking this drastic step? Did she ask for help? I wondered if she had ever been able to be honest, and what she did for self-care.

And of course, when I ask these questions, I am talking to myself.

Talking to myself so much that, finally, I started to listen. I couldn't ask these questions of my sister without being able to answer them myself.

Years of asking all these questions, and hundreds more, hammered into me how cruel suicide can be. It was a cruel thing my sister did. I feel sorry for her misery, whatever it was, but I could not forgive my dead sister for the pain she caused my mother. Not until after they were both dead, only twenty-one months apart. My mother died in a car accident, but part of me feels she died of a broken heart. She certainly died with one.

———

AFTER BREAKFAST, Heather and I take Dad for a drive.

We trick Dad to get him into Heather's car. He doesn't even have shoes on.

"Don't worry about it," Heather tells him. "Slippers are fine. You've never seen my car before, have you Stephen? Get in, let's go for a drive."

Heather takes a different back route to Valley Regional that throws Dad off a bit. He does not seem worried when we drive up to the hospital. His mood has turned passive and accepting. On some level, he must know something is wrong. In the last few days, he has been speeding towards a cliff. Now he has decided to surrender.

Heather pulls up to the Emergency entrance.

"I'll go get a wheelchair," I say.

8

SNOWFLAKES & SNOWMEN

*2 Person Assist: A measure of mobility function;
a 2 person assist means patient requires two people to
assist with transfers or ambulation.*

THE EMERGENCY DEPARTMENT is not that busy, though more active than I had anticipated for a Saturday morning.

Before long, Dad is on a gurney in an assessment bay.

His vital signs are fine, but the sudden onset of confusion needs to be investigated. Blood work is an ordeal when your veins are ninety-five years old. It's an ordeal just watching Dad wince as the technician pokes and prods.

"I'll have to use the baby needle," she says, rummaging in her tray.

Do not start thinking about babies and hospitals and needles. Seriously—just don't.

A doctor comes by to examine my father. I recognize this doctor from when I brought my brother to Emergency.

"Who's this?" the doctor asks Dad, nodding towards me.

Dad peers at me, as if he has just noticed me standing there next to the gurney.

"I know him," Dad says, "but I don't know who he is."

The last time I was in this emergency room was just one year ago, with my brother shaking with fever. Last October. Our mother's birthday.

That same night Harley, the homeless man, was killed, set on fire as he slept in his rough bed at the bus shelter. The town now has plans for a little memorial park across the street from the rebuilt bus stop, near the funeral home.

Sitting in this same emergency room, this time with my father, brings back the ominous yawning—the looming edge of the abyss in that horrible night. But still, imagine that, a town that builds a memorial park to honour its one homeless person.

Emergency rooms are all about patience. Little flurries of activity are separated by long periods of waiting.

While waiting with Dad, I try to participate in his inner world. As murky and opaque as it might be, I try to see deeper.

"Cockroaches," he says. "So many cockroaches in the horse-shoe."

Pointing. "What kind of bees are those?"

He hears a noise: "Somebody sawing wood in the dark." Then decides: "It's all done."

At one point, he becomes quite passionate and speaks directly to me. He really wants me to hear this. "Stay away from the deep end of the pond. Are you listening to me?" He is emphatic. "The deep end!"

At times, he is almost conversational.

"We've had quite an exciting day," he says, pleasantly, as if we have been on a nice drive along the Bay of Fundy instead of making an expedition to Emergency. "Do you know the way home from Kentville now?"

The hospital is just outside of Kentville, and I've known my way home from Kentville for about fifty years.

"Did you bring back the baseball bat?" he asks.

"Yes," he says, "it's been quite a day."

He turns his head and points. "There's a cat here!"

"I wish there was," I say. Honestly, I do. A nice cat is just what I need right now. There should be such things as emergency room cats.

"I wish there was a cat, Dad," I say, wistful and open.

He looks around. "Don't know where it went."

His eyes settle on me, sitting there next to him. "Are we going home now?"

"We're waiting for the doctor," I say. That's the best thing about hospitals—everything can be blamed on the doctor.

"I wish I had brought my underwear."

"Which underwear is that?"

"The winter ones."

It is October. Dad is already in his winter underwear.

During the check-in at Emergency I asked Heather to help me get Dad's wallet so I could find his health care card. I still have his wallet to keep it safe. I realize Dad is probably carrying a jackknife or small box cutter, which he always keeps handy. I'm sure the hospital staff does not want a delusional patient equipped with a knife.

"Do you have your knife, Dad?"

He looks at me, and grunts yes.

"Can you give it to me, please? I'll keep it for you."

He digs in his pocket and hands it over.

Thank you, Dad, for being so agreeable at that moment.

Dad's becoming increasingly agitated on the gurney. He wants to move to the chair, he says, pointing off to his right side.

There is no chair to his right; in fact, there is no chair anywhere in sight.

Dad insists he wants to sit in his chair. I realize he is expressing a kind of muscle memory. If he were at home, lying down in the daytime, he would be on the chesterfield, and his chair would be off to his right. That is where he keeps pointing. He's pointing at his memory of the chair. He is living almost entirely in his head, in his routines, in the mental geometry of home. He is not in this gurney, not in an assessment bay in the emergency department of Valley Regional, but on the chesterfield in his living room. And he wants to move to his chair.

He's creating enough fuss that a nurse finds a reclining chair on wheels and rolls it over. Just give him what he wants, seems to be her motto. We help Dad move to the chair and he settles in, glad for the change. He is calm again, though still confused. He starts to say something but never gets past the first syllable.

The initial tests show that Dad's sodium levels are too low. This can cause hallucinations. All this commotion because of too little salt is bitterly ironic. For years, Dad has been on a low-salt diet because of his high blood pressure. Since much of his food is fresh from a garden and cooked without salt, the pendulum must have swung too far the other way. Conscientiously steering him away from his cheap frozen pepperoni Pizza Pockets has brought him to this—hallucinating.

The good news is that if they bring his salt levels back up, much of his decline may be reversible. The bad news is that he is ninety-five, so it is unclear how much he might be able to bounce back. He is to be admitted to the hospital and kept on intravenous sodium.

By now it's late afternoon and my brother arrives to pick me up and sign whatever is necessary. We've been in touch all day by text, but he's busy working with a carpenter renovating Dad's greenhouse. There is no point in both of us sitting with Dad in Emergency.

Dad's greenhouse is his baby. He still visits it almost every day. Or at least, lately, gets his care worker to go to the greenhouse. It is where he pampers his peanut plants in the spring. There's not much in there these days except some long-suffering aloe vera, a massive jade tree that has taken to blossoming, and thick, scraggly, unrecognizable mounds of orchids that never bloom anymore.

Dad used to do so much in that greenhouse. He grew a pineapple and had his picture in the paper: "Local Man Grows Pineapple." Took two years to grow that pineapple. The paper with his pineapple story is still somewhere in the house, probably in the living room near Dad's chair. The magazine rack next to his chair is laden with his most important paper relics, as well as many things he has no idea why he is saving. He tells me not to throw away anything from the rack and I don't.

Dad built the greenhouse himself, and it was geothermal and solar and sustainable. People talked like that in the 1970s in *Harrowsmith*, a country living magazine, and Dad was a subscriber. Come to think of it, he was basically a hippie—of the conservative variety. What is the word for right-wing hippie?

Dad bragged his greenhouse only cost ten dollars a year to heat, and maybe so, back in the day, when it was intact and tended to religiously. That is—before he started leaving windows open all night with the electric heaters blasting.

The greenhouse was falling apart. Repairs had been postponed for years, and were urgently needed if the greenhouse was going to survive another winter. Getting Dad to agree to these repairs has been one of my achievements on this trip. He knew the greenhouse needed work, but his plan had been to fix it himself. In the meantime, no one else could touch it.

The greenhouse was the one last place where my father was in control. It was his and his alone. His beloved greenhouse was my father's truest home. He would clean and sweep in the greenhouse, but never in the kitchen.

My father and his greenhouse were both in a state of decline, an intermediate stage, heading for eventual ruin. The greenhouse, at least, could be fixed.

In the assessment bay at Emergency, my brother takes out his phone to show Dad a picture.

"What's that?" Dad asks.

"Your greenhouse."

"Is it done?"

"She's tight."

"Good."

My brother showing Dad a picture of his greenhouse while he lay on a gurney in Emergency was an emotional scene between these two men. There was the edge of a crack in my brother's voice when he said, "She's tight." He had been working on the repairs for some time, and drove to Halifax to pick up special double-paned plastic panels designed for energy-efficient greenhouses. He and the carpenter spent the last two days removing the old sloping translucent wall, replacing the rotten framing, and installing the new panels. It was a big job and my brother was proud to show Dad the photo. This was a tender quiet moment, a powerful unspoken exchange.

I often joke about the book I will write titled *If Men Could Talk*, with the subtitle *This Is What They Would Say*. But the truth is that men do talk, in terse little two- and three-word sentences, and leave most everything important unsaid. There can't be much of a book in that. My book will have to be pure fiction.

As it turns out, the upcoming winter is one of the harshest in years. Storms repeatedly dump several feet of snow. That old greenhouse was repaired just in time. It would never have survived the weight of all that snow.

On Sunday morning I arrive at the hospital and find Dad in an observation wing. He already looks like he has been hospitalized for weeks. He's wearing a blue johnny shirt patterned with dark snowflakes and seems very tired.

There is an IV installed in the back of one hand.

The other hand and both arms are bruised and blooming dark purple-yellow. He's been through the wringer.

He looks right at me but seems defeated, resigned.

"How are you, Dad?"

"I'm still here," he says.

He appears feeble, and gaunt, like he has already lost weight. Maybe it's just because he's not wearing his glasses and his teeth are in a container beside his bed. He is a little more coherent. The frenzy is gone, but in its place is weakness.

A whole crew assembles to transfer Dad to a bed in a ward.

They wheel Dad over to the ward and line up his old bed next to his new one. About six people assist in this process, which is slick, efficient, and safety conscious.

They roll Dad on his side to slide a transfer board under him. His hospital gown is open in the back and the transfer board is cold hard plastic.

When the cold board touches his bare flesh, Dad panics like he has been exposed to open flame. "Take it away! Take it away!"

"Just a moment, Stephen," a nurse says.

They slide him onto the board, lift him over to the new bed, and remove the board. No more than a few seconds. Dad's shivering and very upset by the touch of the cold.

Dad's momentary discomfort is something I find amusing. I know, right? What is wrong with me? I'm reasonably empathetic (honestly, I'm probably above average on the empathy scale). And yet a cold board touching my poor old father's bare back makes me secretly smile. I'll tell my brother this story later, framing it as an example of me being cruel and weird, because I know he will enjoy it, too.

Dad is very diligent against the cold. Diligent in his own way—which is to say, erratic. He won't wear a hat, except a trucker's cap. A mesh cap in winter! In every other way he is a fanatic about keeping warm. He cuts the cuffs off big woolly socks and wears these fraying old sock cuffs on each wrist. His shirts must have long sleeves, and by this he means shirts really must have long sleeves. Full-length sleeves, he calls them. He wears two pairs of long underwear (and only thinks it is necessary to wash the inner pair, if that is not too much information). His thick wool socks are worn over one pair of long underwear and underneath the second pair. Cold feet is a favourite topic of conversation. He'll wear winter boots in the house, laced up so tight his feet sweat until the circulation is cut off, and then he complains his feet are cold. Drafts in the house were another battleground. Dad can feel the slice of a cold draft no one else can perceive. That's why the curtains at the top of the stairs are such a big deal, but I am not going to get into that.

The emergency room doctor brought up the topic of medical intervention. How much did we want to do? Does Dad have a DNR, a do-not-resuscitate order? I told him Dad said he didn't want to be resuscitated. I mean, the poor guy is ninety-five—how much are you going to put him through? Just to spend a few more miserable months in hospital?

Don't worry—I didn't say all that. I just said, "Do not resuscitate, my brother has the power of attorney."

The plain fact is 108 billion people have been born on this planet, and most of them have already died. Dad can too.

Later, after Dad was admitted to the hospital, the doctor he is assigned seems offended when I bring up the DNR.

"There's no need to talk about that at this point," he says, looking at me with fresh interest—like, *Who's this guy who wants to push his father into the grave?*

Has my ninety-five-year-old father's condition improved to such a degree that now a DNR cannot possibly be relevant?

The doctor doesn't say much—it's just the way he looked at me.

I don't say anything either. I don't protest my innocence, don't point out another doctor had initiated this conversation.

There is even a chance I may have read too much into the moment of the busy doctor's glance.

I keep thinking about *The Ballad of Narayama*, a Japanese movie set in a timeless village where life is earthy, brutal, and harsh. Closely bound to the cycles of nature, the villagers must follow seasonal customs. Just before the arrival of the snow, in the fall of each year, elders who have turned seventy are carried by their children to the mountain to die.

Was yesterday's trip in Heather's car carrying my father to the mountain?

Dad dozes off in his new bed in the ward and I look around. It is much too early for visitors, but the staff don't seem to care that I'm already here. I do my best to stay out of their way.

Dad is in a room with five other beds. His bed is one of two placed next to the wall of windows. The autumn leaves in the garden quietly speak of fall.

Dad suddenly wakes up and starts feeling around him on the bed.

"What are you looking for?" I ask.

"The queen of hearts."

"Yeah, that would be good to have." Is he dreaming about playing hearts?

"One of the girls must have taken it with her." He settles back, abandoning his search.

A nurse swings by to check on Dad. After she leaves, Dad asks, "Is she going to take me home?"

He wants to go home and it wrings my heart every time he brings it up. It also reminds me of how his father was, for his last few years. Looking for a home that did not exist, or was lost, and he was unable to find it. Not in his head, and not anywhere else.

My father built his house right next to where his parents lived in their sprawling Victorian with the bay windows. The house that I love. And miss. And still dream about.

When Dad's father was getting on, we'd get a phone call: "Old Mr Ilsley walked by. He's headed north on Shaw Road."

Dad would hop in his truck, usually taking one of us boys. My brother remembers this better than I do.

Dad would find his father and offer him a lift. "Where are you going?" Dad asked.

"Home," Grampy said. "I'm heading home," and he'd gesture vaguely, somewhere out there ahead of us. My grandfather was born across the street from the house he lived in. No one knew where he thought he was going when he took off to go home.

Dad could not head straight back or Grampy got upset. They'd have to drive around in circles until his father was satisfied, and then they could complete their journey.

As I stand by my father's hospital bed, I squeeze his hand, and then keep holding on. We are holding hands. His skin feels cool and papery. His hands used to be rough and callused, and never gentle. He lost the last joint of his right thumb when an apple barrel fell on his hand; if Dad touched me at all, it was to drive the hard stump of his thumb into a tender spot by my knee. This fucking hurt, but Dad thought it was great fun.

Dad becomes aware of the warmth of contact and glances down to see who is holding his hand. He looks up at me with surprise when he realizes. He pulls his hand away, as if to scratch his nose, and his hand flops back, like a cat's tail, in a new place.

Unlike a cat's tail, I do not reach for it again.

Back at the house the reality hits me. My father is in the hospital. This is Sunday afternoon, and I'm supposed to leave for Vancouver on Tuesday morning.

Sitting at the dining room table, all by myself, an upswell of emotion rises from the murky depths and a wave hits me hard. Knocks me under.

I'm racked by sudden, hard sobs.

This powerful wave sweeps me along, and when it recedes I am in a new place. All is now clear.

I cannot leave with Dad in the hospital. Tuesday is too soon. I cannot go. I don't know if there is anything I can really do here, but I know I am not ready to leave.

I talk to my brother, and then make phone calls to Vancouver. I reach my boss at his home. He is kind and understanding. All of us baby boomers, we have all lost or are losing our parents. "Do whatever you have to do," he says.

I change my flight.

I'm here until next Wednesday, an additional eight days.

When my brother and I returned to the house from Emergency on Saturday (was that only last night?) we entered a cold, quiet, and empty shell. My brother already had the heat turned down, but my father's domineering presence resonated even in his absence.

I prepared a simple meal and automatically set Dad's place at the table, before I realized. I don't even know exactly what I realized, but I do know my brother and I were both very solemn. We did not speak. Tears were too close, and words would have only encouraged them.

Even if Dad bounces back, he's still ninety-five years old. There is only one way this story is going to turn out.

The end felt suddenly near, and our father's absence was everywhere around us, like the overwhelming vastness of outer space.

Sunday evening my brother and I visit Dad. There is not much to say or do. He is mostly dozing, looking like a wreck of himself. When he is awake he picks at the IV, and has already managed to pull it out. The challenge then is to find another spot to accept the needle. They may have to let go of the idea of giving intravenous sodium.

We do not stay that long. Even a short visit takes the best part of two hours, counting the drive.

I do not know how my brother will juggle his busy life, plus have his father in the hospital.

"As much as possible," I say, "let me do the hospital visiting while I'm still here."

When we get back to the house, the first thing I do is go up the stairs and take down those blasted calf-shit yellow curtains. Yet as a measure of how much residual power Dad still wields, I don't throw them away. I hide them. If Dad comes back and declares war, the missing curtains will still be on hand to put back up, as dirty and tattered and dangerous and inconvenient as they are.

The hospital physiotherapist evaluates Dad and, according to the sign placed at the head of his bed, assesses him as "2 person assist."

Dad is not a liar, exactly, because he believes what he is saying during the assessment. He is trying to tell the truth but simply does not remember.

"Have you ever fallen, Stephen?"

"No," he says.

"He fell twice, just on Friday night. And before that, several times."

Dad turns his head to look at me. I think he'd forgotten I existed, yet here I still am, bedevilling him. However, he doesn't protest my information.

Three days ago, Dad refused my offer of a cane and an arm to lean on. He refused to use a walker. The fierce energy that was driving him, the fire of denial, has collapsed. He is now considered not even capable of using a walker by himself.

The physiotherapist and her assistant make their daily rounds and charm Dad out of his bed for "just one walk around the block."

At Dad's age and condition, if he stops moving, he's done for. Even one lap around the nursing station is better than nothing. He uses a walker, the physio team walks beside him each holding an arm, or at least ready to grab him, and I follow them with one of those recliner chairs on wheels, just in case he suddenly has to sit.

I was worried, recently, that Dad had been teetering on the brink of a great precipice, without even the sense to hold on to the handrail.

Now he has indeed fallen. Maybe not completely off the cliff, but he has slid a long ways down a very slippery slope.

I cry on the phone, talking to a friend, looking out the window near Dad's bed. The view of the autumn landscape shelters me. There are six elderly people in the room with me, but I feel alone, free to whisper unheard. Dad is sleeping, and the others seem oblivious.

Whispering is all my voice, choked with tears, can manage. I feel so guilty for taking Dad to the hospital. "I tricked him," I say. "I brought him here. He would never have come if he knew what I was doing. He trusted me, and I lied to him. Now he's covered with bruises and all he wants is to go home."

———

THE EXTRA DAYS KIND OF BLUR FOR ME HERE. I spend several hours at the hospital, either in one visit, or make two shorter visits. And when I say shorter, I mean at least a couple of hours each.

Basically, I spend all day at the hospital or on the road driving.

I rarely feel useful on these visits, but I do help answer questions. So many different hospital departments come by requesting the same information.

I wonder how Dad would manage all these questions on his own. Don't all old people lie their asses off? They minimize, they deny, they confabulate. Or—they simply forget.

"Do you need help going to the bathroom, Stephen?"

"No," he says.

This man is unable to get out of bed unassisted, much less walk across the room.

"Do you have trouble swallowing?"

"No," he says.

This man eats so fast and thoughtlessly the girls have to cut up all his food into tiny bits just to slow him down. He also needs water with meals, or he starts choking. He claims to have a pocket in his throat that catches food. If he starts to choke, one gets to experience the gross spectacle of him staggering to the sink, hacking and gagging, loudly clearing his throat and horking up great slimy gobs with an exuberance that, even if you only hear it and don't see it, will wash you with shivers of disgust and leave you unable to finish your lunch.

We had a guest for dinner a while ago, and perhaps as a courtesy Dad bypassed the nearby kitchen sink and took his dramatic and sickening performance into the bathroom. Even so, the guest was startled by the noise of cascades of phlegm flooding from the bathroom and asked, "Is he all right?" Her concern was enough to make my brother and me realize just how much we had learned to blur out what Dad was doing, and how disgusting and possibly alarming it really was.

"He's fine," my brother said.

"He does that all the time," I said. "It's totally gross, and then he'll come back and eat even more."

One of my little missions at the dining room table is to remind Dad to chew what he has in his mouth, to swallow what he is chewing, and to swallow everything before shovelling any more food into his gaping maw.

The girls never leave him alone during meals. They watch him like hawks. It says to do this right in Dad's care manual that lives on top of the fridge.

The dietician asks, "Any issues with eating or swallowing, Stephen?"

"No," he says. "I eat well."

Dad requires assistance with his lunch at the hospital. He has trouble identifying what things are because everything is unfamiliar.

"This is meatloaf and mashed potatoes," I say. "And that is gravy in the cup."

Dad decides the gravy must be a beverage. He picks up the cup and takes a swig.

"You can do that Dad, or you can pour it over your mashed potatoes." (*And make a big mess*, is what I think but do not say.)

Some of the items are in containers that Dad does not have the dexterity to open. I peel the foil lid off a tub of applesauce. As a third-generation son of the Apple Capital of Nova Scotia, I cannot help but feel annoyed and perplexed to see that my father's little tub of applesauce, purchased by Canadian taxpayers, is labelled, *Product of China*.

I arrive at the hospital and Dad is more alert. "Good morning," he says.

"How are you, Dad?"

"Pretty well worn out," he says.

"Well that's to be expected, considering."

He squints at me. "Is that my jacket?" he says, indicating the sweater I have on.

"Yes."

"No wonder I can't find it."

The sweater is a plain grey cardigan, light wool, with mother-of-pearl buttons. He thinks it's "too nice," so he never wears it. I guess he was saving it for a special occasion.

I'm wearing it under my jacket. It's cold sitting around hospitals. It's mine now.

Later that morning I'm hovering near the nursing station, eyeing one of the doctors filling out a chart. This doctor looks very much like a friend from Vancouver, a specialist, who had moved to Nova Scotia. When she spots me, she says my name with an exclamation mark, gives me a big hug, and insists on calling her partner so the three of us can go for lunch.

This all happens in front of everyone at the nursing station.

When I return to the hospital after lunch, Dad has been moved to a private room.

The nurse says he had diarrhea and had to be isolated, but I wonder. It seems like quite a coincidence.

I don't know how many times I explain to Dad how to use the call button. If he asks me to fetch a nurse, I tell him to push the button.

When he finally starts pushing the button without a prompt, I'm curious. "What do you want, Dad?"

"Bathroom."

"Someone will be here soon."

He keeps asking me to help him to the bathroom. I always say, "Push the button." I don't have the training to help him; plus, we know what can happen if I try. These nurses are skilful and experienced. Dad is putty in their hands. With me, he argues and fights. As much as I want to help, I have to accept that sometimes I only make things worse.

The nurses get Dad up and dressed in the morning and seated in the large comfy chair next to the bed. Over his lap is an incongruously gaudy fleece blanket with cartoon snowmen I've brought from home. When he's in the chair, the nurse slides a tray in front of him, so he can eat his lunch or pretend to do the crossword puzzle. It takes Dad a day or so to realize this tray also prevents him from leaving the chair.

He is tray-locked.

When he discovers this, the wild look flickers back into his face. He is trapped, and pissed, with barely enough energy to express his frustration. It's good that he has come around enough to recognize that he is trapped. It is also very upsetting for him to come around enough to recognize that he is trapped.

He bitterly resents being locked in the chair and argues with the nurses about this. At first, they insist, for his own good, but as he slowly regains his cognition, and with me there with him, they don't lock him in but make him promise not to leave the chair without calling someone. The chair is alarmed, so they would know if he got up on his own.

The problem is that he does not remember his limitations. He will attempt to get up and go somewhere without assistance. When I'm there, I remind him to push the button and wait for a nurse. "Don't try to get up, Dad," I say. "Call the nurse." His bed and the chair are both alarmed, but he is at risk. He's just strong enough to try to do something and end up hurting himself.

"I don't want to bother the nurses," he says. "Why won't you help me?"

In his private hospital room, Dad and I have more freedom to explore quiet moments.

In one such lull, I broach a looming topic. Some people consider me morbid, because this is just the sort of discussion I will initiate.

Some people would rather poke needles in their eyes than ask an important question.

"Are you afraid of dying?"

"No," Dad says, his response quite matter-of-fact.

He considers a moment and then looks at me with his old, watery eyes. "Am I dying?"

"Not that I know of."

"Okay." He accepts my answer.

"But Dad—you are ninety-five. It's going to happen sometime. None of us knows when. This year, five years, who knows?"

"I'm not afraid," he says. "I'm not worried."

I believe him.

"I wouldn't want much more like this," he says.

I totally believe him.

Dad has already told me he wants to be cremated. He wants his ashes scattered in the garden "so I can be with your mother." We've talked about his funeral, and if there is a minister in particular that he likes (there isn't). My brother is our father's executor, but they have never talked about Dad's final wishes.

Over the last few years I have sat with Dad for hours in his living room, and I ask direct questions. And follow-up questions.

I have always been the nosy one.

———

DAD HAS A NEW TRICK, and he does it well. He meows. It is very convincing. He meows a lot now. He likes to tease the nurses, make them come looking for the cat.

Even before he came to the hospital, he could get a reaction from his care workers with his mimicry. He meows, and then he laughs, delighted with himself.

As his words have been sliding away just out of reach, he is meowing to prove, I think, that he still has something to say.

Dad's focus and awareness wavers in and out. Sometimes he's surprisingly sharp, other times out of it.

"Are there three birds in here?" he asks.

"I need to go home," he says. "How will the doctor find me?"

"I lost my wallet," he says. "There was three hundred dollars in it."

"I have your wallet, Dad. It's okay. I'm keeping it safe for you."

And he was absolutely right. There is $300 in it. Despite everything he has gone through, he knows exactly how much money was in his wallet last Saturday.

"Is it freezing over there yet?" he asks me, concerned.

"Over where?"

"Over in the bed yet?"

"No," I say, just because I feel this is the reassuring answer. It is October. It is probably a gardening question.

And so my extra week passes like this, at the hospital. Phoning the day program to say Dad will not be coming on Friday. Yes, I will let them know if anything changes. Shuttling Dad's laundry back and forth so he has clean clothes to wear. Reading books from the gift shop book exchange (*The Bridges*: "A haunting novel of human passions by Scandinavia's greatest modern author"). Watching Dad sleep, his mouth wide open. Remembering sitting with my grandmother, Dad's mother, when she lived alone after Grampy died. She would slip into a nap in her chair, snoring away, and then completely stop breathing. I sat there, a teenager, watching over my grandmother, wondering if she had taken her last breath. Doing the same thing now with her son, my father, as he sleeps and his breathing pauses, and pauses, and pauses—and then the gulp of air.

Sitting there next to him, thinking of his mother and picking away at the crossword puzzle from the paper. I bring the paper for Dad, because that was a big part of his daily routine, glancing at the newspaper and working on the puzzles.

But he is not doing the crossword or the sudoku in the hospital.

"When do we get back to where we're staying?" he asks, suddenly awake.

There is, of course, a last scene with Dad in the hospital, tray-locked in his chair, him confused and me sad. Wondering if this is the last time, as I have wondered so many times, with increasing levels of certainty.

I've been expecting my father's death for twenty years, and going through waves of grief, of anticipatory loss, of gratitude and sorrow. Waves of the stages of grief and ending up at acceptance. Accepting what is and what will be. Accepting the inevitable.

I've wondered so many times, but this time sure looks especially grim.

There is a theory Dad and I never bonded because the summer of my birth he had breast cancer, and was in hospital in Halifax. To treat the cancer he underwent a radical mastectomy. When he returned home, he never picked me up or held me. He was too sore. Imagine my mother at this time, with me as a howling newborn and two other small children, no money, and her husband in hospital a hundred miles away. And then, when my father does return home, he is someone else for my mother to take care of.

There is another theory my mother was incredibly stressed the whole time she was carrying me, and this is why I was born a crybaby—exposed in the womb to all she was going through and swimming in a sea of anxiety.

I used to cry all the time. Some people would claim I still do.

Dad had all those cancer treatments when I was an infant, but I have no memory of ever seeing him in a hospital. Despite all his complaints, he's never really been sick. But now he looks diminished and defeated, so lost and old, locked there in his chair reaching into the air, his attention wavering.

He has been asking when I leave.

"Wednesday," I say. "Wednesday," he repeats.

"Three more days," I say. "Two more days."

"Wednesday," he says.

He doesn't realize until the last minute that me leaving Wednesday means the last day I see him will be Tuesday. It is now Tuesday, and time for me to go.

"Will I see you again?" he asks. Such a loaded question.

"I'm sorry," I say. "I have to go to the airport in the morning."

"Okay," he says.

The colourful fleece blanket over his legs swims—blurry snowmen with carrot noses, green plaid scarves, and bright red hats.

"I could drop by in the morning for a few minutes. It's on the way."

"No," he says, "that's okay. You have a long drive."

We say a brief goodbye.

We do not touch.

I do not want to cry like a baby.

I am sure he would not want me to do that, either. He's already had to live through it once. A second time would probably kill him.

Not far from the hospital, along Brooklyn Street, I see a hawk flying by the side of the road, swooping low.

"Thank you for showing yourself," I say.

The sight of the hawk thrills me, and I wonder if there is a message.

This was the last time I saw my father. I want to say I suspected this, but for years every time I said goodbye, I wondered if I would see my father again. This was the first time he was in the hospital when I left. And that hospital was the last place I saw him.

We had just said goodbye.

And the hawk swooped low next to me, suspended above eternity, as I drove away.

9

LAST CALL

*If birth is a kind of forgetting, could dying be a
kind of remembering?*

—Eve Joseph, *In the Slender Margin:
The Intimate Strangeness of Death and Dying*

*When we realize that life is the expression of death and death is
the expression of life, that continuity cannot exist without disconti-
nuity, then there is no longer any need to cling to one and fear the
other. There is no longer any ground for the brave or the cowardly.*

—Chögyam Trungpa, *The Heart of the Buddha*

IT'S APRIL, A MONDAY, AND I'M AT WORK. I play a guessing game
with a friend at the office who will kill me if I write about him. Our
game is called "Guess Who Died Today?" This game started with
the young actor Heath Ledger, whose premature death came as a
big shock, but you can count on people to die with great regularity,
so the game is always fresh.

"Do you know who died today?" I ask.

"Yes, Günter Grass."

"And who else?" I ask.

"Um, dunno. Haven't heard."

"My father," I say, largely just mouthing the f-word.

"What?! Why didn't you say something?"

"My brother phoned me this morning. He waited until seven, my time. He felt there was no reason to wake me in the middle of the night."

This is the first time I have told anyone the news of my father's death.

I don't tell anyone else at work because I don't want to be fussed over.

Just before the end of the workday, my boss walks into my office.

"I've been meaning to ask," he says. "How's your father doing?"

"Well, actually, he died this morning."

My boss says, "I'm not surprised, considering."

From the time I fly away with the hawk, leaving my father in the hospital, to the time of his death is less than six months. This is an entire phase of Dad's decline that I do not witness. It involves more hours of care workers at the house. A hospital bed is installed in what was the den, which had finally been emptied and fixed up so it could be quickly turned into a main-floor bedroom.

There are two or three trips back to the hospital by ambulance. There are rallies and setbacks. There are many phone calls and texts between Nova Scotia and Vancouver.

I plan a trip for April.

My father dies the day before I am due to arrive.

My ego wants Dad to have waited to see me, to hang on for one last dramatic scene, with violins, a soaring score, and a neat resolution.

Yeah, that would have been nice.

If only the whole world revolved around me.

If only my ego would have been satisfied with just that.

Several years ago a dream helped me peer into the roiling depths of my relationship with my father:

Woke up early with a dream of my father. He was holding me from behind, like we were standing. He was behind me and his arms were around me. Around my shoulders in a nice way, and he was saying he loved me. He took a solemn moment to express his feelings, and it was totally heartwarming. I was glowing inside.

But also, even though this is something I've always wanted—it was not good enough.

Why are you telling me now? I wanted to know. I questioned his timing. I wanted to know why, after some forty years, he finally expressed something.

No matter what my father did it would not have been enough—that is the takeaway from this vision. I'm wishing for something impossible. He says he loves me, and I say, "So what? Why are you telling me now? Why didn't you tell that lonely boy forty years ago?"

A dream can be wish-fulfillment, but wish-fulfillment can serve to demonstrate that what you think you want will not satisfy. The message in this dream is that I could not expect my father to fix the way I feel.

Ultimately he is not the problem.

I am.

You cannot fill a bottomless hole. The practical approach when confronting the bottomless pit is to embrace emptiness. Make the hole whole.

Emptiness is the most common translation of the Sanskrit word "*shunyata.*" The English word "emptiness" conveys many meanings and is not an entirely adequate translation. The essence of *shunyata* also embodies qualities of boundlessness, openness, and transparent interdependence.

When we let go, something is born. And what is born when we let go is spacious and boundless—the rich freedom of "emptiness."

Even if it exists only for a fleeting moment, the boundlessness is always there.

That is why we pause, why we sit and breathe—to feel the openness of space.

In the documentary *Griefwalker*, Stephen Jenkinson says that the twin of grief is the love of life. Grief only exists because of a love of life. So—is grief a problem, or the reward? Grief is a necessary part of the emotional equation if one is to have a passion for life. In the mind math of the Buddhists, every emotion equals suffering if there is attachment, or clinging.

Now that he is gone, and I have returned to my life, I see Dad everywhere.

I see him in the outside world.

I see him shuffle into the SkyTrain station.

I see him in every person with a walker, or a cane.

An older Asian man during my morning commute screens my projection. There are many elderly Asians who push onto the bus at Main Street–Science World and go only two stops to Chinatown. This neat little gent is no bigger than a minute, as my mother used to say, and propels himself forward with an upright rigid posture, his weight maybe too far back on his heels. His progress is slow, but his tiny little steps shuffle quickly.

He ignores the reserved seats at the front of the bus. "Those seats are for the old people," I imagine him saying, in my father's voice.

He progresses the length of the long articulated bus, glaring at any commuter who dares offer their seat. Bus drivers always wait for this old man to sit down, and that tells you something. They always wait for him. The whole bus waits. A whole busload of cranky impatient morning commuters pauses—and waits for this old man to slowly quickstep the entire length of the double-long bus and select a seat near the back.

He reminds me so much of my father, this elderly Asian man. The shuffling little steps, of course, but also the stubborn refusal to accept himself as old. The anger at any expression of kindness that might mark him as feeble. The lack of personal insight, and flickering self-awareness. He might feel the whole world is against him, without realizing how much kindness is nearby, not noticing a whole busload of people waiting, and waiting, for him to find the place where he feels most comfortable for his two-block journey.

I was sleeping in the spare room, and needed to pee.

I felt my way into the bathroom between the spare room and Dad's bedroom and flicked on the light.

The compact fluorescent bulbs took a moment to come alive, and by then I was at the sink. Light flared up and there, looming out the darkness, was Dad, sitting on the toilet.

I reeled back with a yelp, clutching at my heart.

He had been sitting there in the dark, one hand between his legs, his sleepwear tugged down to his knees. Surprisingly thin thighs glowed ghostly white in the sudden harsh light.

"Scared you, did I?" His voice, toothless, was hollow and slurred.

I never used that bathroom in the nighttime again. I went to the main floor, one flight down, to the new bathroom, which was bright enough from the street lights that I didn't need to illuminate the fishbowl.

The sudden flaring image of my father was seared into my retinas, and lingers in my perception. In the residual blinding glare, my father inhabits every darkness, poised to spring into view.

My father becomes superimposed on everything I look at. Even the darkness. He could be sitting quietly in any dark room, just waiting for me to flip the switch.

Everywhere around me in Vancouver, I sense my father's presence. Everywhere I look, everywhere I imagine.

"Why are you here?" I ask.

"Why not?" he answers.

When I look down, I see my father's legs in my jeans.

I see his face in my mirror when I shave.

I see him in the way my tongue works in my mouth when I'm using scissors.

I see my father in the vitamins I discover when I sweep my kitchen floor.

I feel him, increasingly, inside me.

I tell a spiritual adviser that I feel my father near me.

"That's nice," she says.

"But," I say, "I don't know if I *want* him around. Isn't there a better place for him to be?"

The Tibetan Buddhists commonly believe that consciousness lingers with the body, or in this plane, and can take forty-nine days to travel through the bardos and into a new life.

In *Living Is Dying: How to Prepare for Dying, Death and Beyond*, Dzongsar Jamyang Khyentse explains: "'Bardo' is a Tibetan word that means 'in between' and is sometimes translated as 'intermediate state.' To put it very simply, a bardo is what lies in between two illusory boundaries. For example, this very moment lies between the boundaries of the past and the future; in other words, today lies between yesterday and tomorrow. At the same time, we must always remember that everything is an illusion, including the bardos, so there are no truly existing borders dividing the past from the present or the present from the future. This is important."

Forty-nine days may be just a convention, but at the end of that period, in early June, I have a modest ceremony for my father. I light a candle in front of his photo. I pray for him to be at peace, to move into the light. I pray for my father without really knowing what I am praying for. I am just praying for my father. I ask Guru Rinpoche, Padmasambhava, who brought Buddhist teachings to Tibet, for guidance—even though I don't even know him that well.

Now I only see my father in the things I say, in the way I move, in the sound of my voice in my head.

After I wrote "Bingo and Black Ice" and was preparing to send it to a creative non-fiction contest, encased in a fragile magical bubble of hope and wishful thinking, I asked my mother and my sister for help.

"Okay. Mom? Sandra? It's all you now. You take it from here."

When I returned to Vancouver after my father died and he was all around me, I sent a short story to a fiction contest.

"Okay, Dad," I said. "You want something to do? This one's on you. You won't like the story but there it is. It's mine. How about some help?"

There are so many slices and scenes and memories and stories of my father. All scrambled in my head and around me, outside and inside, like a giant multi-dimensional jigsaw puzzle where the final picture is unknown, and all the pieces may or may not fit.

Some of the pieces may not even belong to this puzzle.

From being tended by care workers, their hours increasing as Veterans Affairs saw fit, Dad naturally soon became a care worker supervisor. He'd had the chance to observe their work habits and could offer many suggestions. He anticipated much of the daily routine.

My father, they all said, was easy to work with.

Dad became so familiar with their jobs that he conceived the notion that he should start working for the same agency. He could be a care worker. Why not? He already knew what to do—he had learned by watching.

Learned on the job, so to speak.

Angela respected what Dad had to say, even if she then steered him in a more realistic direction. She gave every indication of taking Dad's new career suggestion seriously. She listed the job requirements for working at the agency. You need to be available for shift work, you need to be physically fit—so far, Dad saw no obstacles. And you need a car. And a driver's licence. Dad had access to a car, but did not have a licence.

"Oh, too bad," she said.

As a kind of joke, or perhaps as some rather barbed teasing, a couple of times I casually asked Dad this question: "Do you remember the last time you called me?"

He would pause to think about it, but no, he could not remember.

"I remember," I said. "It was 1988."

So we are talking twenty-two, twenty-four, more than twenty-five years ago. The number kept creeping up. More than twenty years without a phone call, a birthday card, or anything from Dad. Oh, he seemed happy enough to hear from me. As he got older he even said things like, "I was hoping it was you" when I called on his birthday. He seemed to want to hear from me, but never picked up the phone and punched my number.

After my mother died, Dad phoned me just twice—on Christmas (three weeks after her death) and a few months later, on my birthday. Mom was always the special lubricating social glue in the family, and when Dad phoned after her death, I thought he was going to step up to the parenting plate. But no. He phoned those two times and that was it for him.

He had done his bit.

And to be fair, it's not like I have a birthday every year. Certainly not anymore. I skip years now, to slow down the count.

Kim heard me talking to Dad about the last time he called me and was scandalized.

"Are you serious?" she said. "1988?"

After I left she decided to do something.

She phoned me in Vancouver and handed the phone to Dad. He did not have much to say, and soon returned the phone to Kim. We had a good natter.

For my birthday that year, Kim got a card for Dad to sign.

Dad's handwriting was showing his age. On the card he wrote, *Happy Birthday* and signed it, *Stephen*.

Then he crossed out *Stephen* and wrote, *oops Dad*.

And then he put my birthday card, in an envelope with a stamp, on the table next to his chair. Where it stayed for about two years until, tidying up the living room after Dad had died, I discovered it under a messy pile of spine-broke crossword puzzle dictionaries. A card addressed to me with the message, in Dad's deteriorated scrawl, *Happy Birthday, oops Dad*.

Is now the time to mention a series of nicknames for me, the youngest in the family? The mistake. The accident.

And the one that stuck—the afterthought.

. If I heard Dad pick up the phone and call someone, I was naturally a little curious, and also felt the pinch of jealousy. With one of his friends he was so polite and courtly I was flabbergasted. I remember telling my brother, "Dad has manners! He can actually be charming. He says things like, 'Nice talking to you.'"

"Oh yeah," my brother said. "If he wants something he can be nice."

Dad mostly called someone when there was something in particular he wanted. He never called just to talk. But does this mean Dad didn't want anything from me? The alternative could have been worse—phoning all the time with problems I had no way to solve. I suppose I am questioning why Dad did not simply want to know how I was. Why didn't he want to say hello? I mean, want it enough to pick up the phone. I phoned no less than twice a year. On his birthday in early January and on Father's Day. Twice a year minimum was pure guilt management.

My father had no problems with guilt management. He never phoned at all. Not since 1988—but perhaps I already mentioned that.

So—he didn't feel guilty. Isn't that a good thing? Remember, please, the dream—no matter what he did, it would not have been enough.

How could my father possibly have been able to satisfy that demanding, emotional, hyper-weird afterthought of a son?

During one of our little performances, Dad and I arrived at a scene where he had to describe the phases of my life. I claimed he knew very little about me, which he emphatically denied.

"Okay," I said, "Where did I go to school?"

"Auburn," he said, obviously proud of himself for knowing this.

Auburn was where my high school was, not the name of the school, but close enough. "And then?"

Now he was less sure and had to think about it. "And then, Acadia."

"Okay, and then?"

Now Dad pounced. He intended to expose my hypocrisy. "And then," he said, "you took off and never told anyone where you went!"

He banged the arm of his chair and settled back, triumphant.

I was stunned by my father's view of me, his youngest child. When I "took off," I went to Toronto to go to law school. My parents bought me a matching set of Naugahyde luggage, ochre with brown straps, and like always, drove me to the airport. There was no mystery. My mother phoned me at least once a week, usually on a weekend morning when I was still asleep. Dad bitched about the phone bills.

During phone calls with my mother I could hear my father whispering in the background. "Long distance!" he hissed, as if Mom did not know what she was doing. He tapped the back of his wrist too, with a finger—I've seen him do that just for talking too long on the phone, never mind long distance.

"Didn't you wonder where I was?" I asked. "When I took off?"

"No one knew how to reach you."

"Did you ever think to ask your wife where I was?" I said. "Mom knew the whole time. She could have told you, if you wanted to know."

It's startling to realize that Dad believed I just took off and disappeared out of their lives. It boils down to this—for him to know where I was or what I was doing was not important. I had nothing he wanted.

My father did not recognize that his "boys" were grown adults, even though we are both obviously middle-aged. He mostly treated us like we were ten-year-olds with adult strength who were eager to work. Sometimes, I would say, "Dad, do you know how old I am?" Right off the top of his head, he had no idea. He would have to do the math, based on some major life event he did pay attention to that roughly coincided with my birth.

I wish I knew for certain what that event was—I could make a funny story out of it. Like, Dad can't remember the year I was born but knows when he was laid up with cancer. So if he wants to know how old I am, he just thinks about cancer and that's close enough.

It never seemed to register with my father that I went to law school. He never asked for free legal advice, or even acknowledged that I might have the tiniest bit of valuable education.

Part of Dad's regular mail concerned a prepaid funeral arrangement run by a co-op. Dad had some idea what his agreement covered, but I asked to see the contract. It was short, written in plain language, and fairly straightforward. I summarized the terms of the agreement, some of which did not align with Dad's recollections.

Someone was visiting Dad, and that is how the topic of prepaid funerals came up. When I went back into the dining room, Dad leaned over towards his friend and lowered his voice.

"Don't listen to him," Dad said. "He doesn't know what he is talking about."

In fact, it is absolutely true that I am completely unqualified to give any sort of legal advice, so maybe Dad was onto something.

During the last years of his life, from 2010 to 2015, thoughts of my father consumed me in a way they never had before. Eldercare is exhausting, frustrating, and profoundly humbling. Attempting to care for Dad forced me to identify with and confront both a battered child and an unflinching, stern adult.

Despite all that happened, after my father died I spend even more time revisiting scenarios and imagining how I could have done better. Perhaps he might still be alive, still relatively healthy, if only I had been a better son.

This must be the bargaining stage of the classic five stages of grief. Anger and denial never happened—I mean in response to my father's death, not with all that magnificent pre-grieving. I've lived with acceptance for a while. Acceptance is strangely mingled now with bargaining. Acceptance is bargaining. Every time I think, *if only* ... acceptance steps up and says, *Get real, Dad was ninety-six. No one lives forever. You can't fix aging.*

My feelings about my father dying—the impulse to negotiate— perhaps run parallel to my father's feelings about his own father. Did Dad feel he should have done more? I wonder how many years Dad walked around thinking, *If only I had insisted they keep my father in his long underwear, he would still be alive.*

Dad's favourite advice as he got older was "Don't get old."

It's fun advice and usually got a sympathetic laugh. But the alternative, really, is "Die young."

I've seen both of these methods of living and dying in action and I have to say—dying young is worse.

Dying young is much worse.

Getting old does require a huge reservoir of patience.

That much can be trying.

Not just for the old person—for all of us.

There's a huge teaching in this process: in patience, in kindness, in forgiveness.

Death is a clarifying event. All the rest, all the distractions, all the petty grievances—it all drops away.

Like the veils from our eyes.

At least—that is the theory.

In *Heart of a Dog*, Laurie Anderson says: "The purpose of death is the release of love."

I talked to my father a few times in his last six months. I phoned him at home in January, on his ninety-sixth birthday, and tried reaching him when he was hospitalized again. I had to call the nursing station first, to see how he was doing, and they would let him know I was about to call. If I tried calling him without any warning, he would not pick up. He said, "I didn't think it was for me."

He always asked, "Where are you?" every time I called.

"Vancouver," I said. I like to think he was hoping I was in Nova Scotia.

He was worried I would come home and miss him, because he was in the hospital. "You might not know where I am."

"Don't worry, Dad. I'll be able to find you. I'll know where you are."

In our last phone call, in late March, his breathing was shallow and laboured.

As was mandatory, we first talked about the weather. Dad claimed there was ten feet of snow. He was joking, but in fact, that particular winter, it was almost true.

"Is there enough room for you and me?" Dad said.

"Where?"

"In Berwick."

"There's plenty of room."

"Let me know if you come here," Dad said. "I'll try to meet you in Berwick."

"I'll let you know, Dad," I said. "Talk to you soon."

"Okay," he breathed. "Bye."

"Bye, Dad." He had already hung up.

This phone call prompted me to stop putting it off and book a plane ticket home to see my father.

———

ON THE DAY BEFORE OUR FATHER'S FUNERAL, my brother sits on the chesterfield and reads "Bingo and Black Ice." After I turned it over to my mother and my sister, "Bingo and Black Ice" won a contest and had just been published.

There is a symmetry here, is there not? Reading something about me coming home for our mother's funeral when I have come home for our father's funeral.

My brother knows the name of our sister's father. "Oh, that's blah-blah," he says. But I don't pay attention and still do not know.

And the hydro pole—he's pretty sure the insurance took care of that.

And you know? Maybe I do remember the name of the movie now—the one where I bawled over the hysterectomy. Took a bit of work to discover and of course the storyline is quite different. Should I even say what I think the movie was? If I do you'll just point out how my recollections are alarmingly loose.

After reading "Bingo and Black Ice" my brother tells me he was angry, too. With our sister. It's been twenty-nine years, but this is the first time we talk about her suicide.

"You don't know what it was like," he says. "Living here with those two, after that. Everyone was miserable. Sometimes I had to leave the table and get out of the house. Couldn't stand it."

He doesn't know who the uncle was who befriended me. Driving up the street, I point to a bungalow. "They were in there. I remember being in that house."

There was an Uncle Lou, my mother's uncle, but my brother has no memory of him being around then, or living just up the street.

It's funny, having that curious uncle appear out of the wood-work when my mother died. No such companionable uncle appears when my father dies—but then again, I don't need one. My father was ninety-six, and in the hospital. My mother's death was a great shock and I was in shock.

And of course, the truth of it is that I have no more great-uncles. Even if I needed one.

I was in shock that first day in Vancouver after getting the phone call from my brother. But by the time I am packing for the trip, something flips inside. I know what to bring, what to expect. I start to feel relieved it is over.

From the outside world in Vancouver to ground zero of my inside world, my father's house in small-town Nova Scotia, door to door, takes about twelve hours. At least I know what I am flying into.

In the middle of April, when I arrive in the Annapolis Valley, snow is piled high next to the roads. Fields are still covered two to three feet deep.

Across the street from my father's house, at the new fire hall built on the land Dad sold to the town several years ago, we have a simple memorial ceremony. The view out the window we sit facing at the service is across the road to my father's garden, glistening in the sun, patches and stalks poking out of the snow. I almost expect to see Dad stomping around the perimeter of his field, kicking at the ice, impatient to be planting.

I had talked to Dad about having a goodbye party for him. Some people think goodbye parties are a great idea. It's like a living wake, and a chance to celebrate a life in the living presence of the person being celebrated.

Dad was skeptical. "Who would we invite?" he asked.

He had a point. Dad had lived so long most of his long-time friends had passed, and the rest were unable to leave their homes.

The goodbye party for Dad did not happen while he was alive, but I wish he could have attended his celebration of life. He touched so many lives. Hundreds of people do not need invitations to show up and talk about Dad. There is one baby, and one man even older than my father. So many people tell me how gentle and kind my father was, always so generous, so very helpful.

And of course, there is quiet, knowing laughter at any mention of peanuts.

The goodbye party never ends.

The goodbye party is a friend for the rest of your life.

After our father's memorial service, my brother and I walk back to what is now my brother's house.

"Well," he says, "you've got another chapter for your book."

So yeah. Thanks, Dad. Thanks for everything.

———

THE FAMILY HOME DID NOT DISAPPEAR ALL AT ONCE. For many years, in fact, it seemed eternal—at least from a distance. It would always be my home and my parents are always my parents. That much is true.

But a mother can die in a car accident and the home becomes less homey. It is still there, but certainly not as clean, and not nearly so emotional.

My own room was a time capsule, just as I left it the last time I visited. Until one day, the room was gone. Not the room, but the contents. The top floor was renovated, reinsulated, and the debris of my adolescence and misspent youth was dispersed, no longer coherent and recognizable.

And then I became an orphan. And at such a tender age. Being orphaned is like being left on the side of road and watching your ride drive away, knowing it will never come back. (Depending where you were dropped off, maybe even worse than that.)

Being an orphan means the faraway family home has even weaker gravity.

And now the family home has been sold. Every piece of it must be handled and face judgment—toss it, keep it, give it away.

Every broken childhood toy, everything crammed in the attic, every taped-up board game. The Mouse Trap game was missing some parts but still workable—what do we do with this?

The emotional content of every item must be weighed.

Every dish my mother touched.

Every piece of paper my father hoarded for decades.

Every detail is fed into the memoir chipper, chopped into tiny symbolic bits, and spewed back out onto the page.

And then the family home will be gone forever.

I'll be a new kind of orphan, a family-homeless orphan.

A family-homeless orphan with a book.

My father's voice calling my name wakes me. I am sleeping in the spare room in my father's house, next to his bedroom.

"George!" I hear.

"Just a minute," I answer. I wonder what he wants. I struggle to come awake.

Then I really do wake up.

I am in my bed in Vancouver.

And my father has been dead for almost two years.

He did call me, after all. This was the last time I heard his voice.

ACKNOWLEDGMENTS

In the last years of his life, my father was blessed by the kindness of many caregivers. I met fifteen, and there were many more. The caregivers in this memoir are composite characters, given made up names, and do not depict individuals.

I wish to thank the taxpayers of British Columbia for supporting the completion of this book through a grant from the BC Arts Council when the project was called *What Next: Not Really a Question*.

This project was also given a boost when my work was selected as the creative non-fiction winner of the 2014 Lush Triumphant Literary Awards. Thanks to Brian Kaufman and the good folks at *subTerrain* magazine for publishing "Bingo and Black Ice."

The truth is that a vast number of people have contributed to this memoir, and I cannot possibly list them all. I hope to repay all of you as best I can.

My brother is not named in this book, but I am extremely grateful for everything he has done. He deserves special thanks for never saying no to this project, even when neither of us had a clue how it might turn out.

GEORGE K. ILSLEY is the author of the story collection *Random Acts of Hatred* and the novel *ManBug*. His stories have also appeared in numerous anthologies and magazines. Selected as a writer-in-residence at Berton House Writers' Retreat in Dawson City, Yukon, George has won the Lush Triumphant Literary Award for creative non-fiction and for fiction. Originally from Nova Scotia, he now lives in Vancouver.